The Evangelical
FORFEIT

John Seel

The Evangelical FORFEIT

Can We Recover?

HOURGLASS BOOKS

Baker Books

A Division of Baker Book House Co
Grand Rapids, Michigan 49516

Scripture quotations taken from the *Holy Bible, New International Version*. Copyright © 1973, 1978, 1984 by International Bible Society.

ISBN 0-8010-8362-1

Printed in the United States of America

Cover by Eric Walljasper

Library of Congress Cataloging-in-Publication Data

Seel, John.
    The Evangelical forfeit : can we recover? / John Seel.
       p.   cm.
    Includes bibliographical references.
    ISBN 0-8010-8362-1
    1. Evangelicalism —United States—History—20th century.
2. Christianity and culture. 3. United States—Church history—20th century. I. Title.
BR1642.U5S44   1993
277.3'0829—dc20   93-14326

To Sue

whose heart and hand
are a gift beyond repaying

CONTENTS

Acknowledgments   9

1 A Time to Rethink   11

2 Yesterday's Man   25

3 The Crises of Evangelicalism   48

4 Playing for Different Stakes   69

5 Reforging a Biblical Identity   104

Notes   118

ACKNOWLEDGMENTS

This book is born of friendship. A. G. Sertillanges writes, "Friendship is an obstetric art; it draws out our riches and deepest resources; it unfolds the wings of dreams and hidden indeterminate thoughts; it serves as a check on our judgments, tries out our new ideas, keeps up our ardor, and inflames our enthusiasm."

To these spiritual and intellectual midwives, I acknowledge my debt and gratitude: to my parents, Dave and Mary Seel; to my two sons, David and Alex; to my colleagues, Os Guinness, Al McDonald, and Peter Edman; and finally to my editor, Amy Boucher. They have each taught lessons of friendship whose value extends far beyond this writing.

1

A TIME TO RETHINK

forfeit (fôr⁄fit) *n.* [ME. *forfet* < OFr. *forfait*, pp. of *forfaire*, to transgress < ML. *forisfacere*, to do wrong, lit., to do beyond < L. *foris*, *foras*, out-of-doors, beyond (see FOREIGN) + *facere* (see FACT)]: something that one loses or has to give up because of some fault or neglect of duty

FACING THE CHALLENGES

AMERICAN EVANGELICALS FACE growing spiritual and cultural trouble. We have forfeited our influence within American society and are on the verge of forfeiting the vestiges of our biblical identity. The signs of this crisis, once veiled by superficial success, are now widely apparent.

In January 1986, the evangelical parachurch ministry, the Navigators, held a consultation on secularization with sixty selected members of its staff in attendance. They met to address criticisms-cum-recommendations from their European branch that their approach to evangelism, based on U.S. methods developed in the 1940s, was no longer effective within the secular European context. The report, "Evangelism, Secularization, and The Navigators," led to a complete conceptual and organizational rethinking of the ministry.

In May 1989, more than three hundred fifty evangelical pastors, theologians, educators, and church officials gathered at

Trinity Evangelical Divinity School in Deerfield, Illinois, to seek consensus on the core beliefs of the evangelical movement. Carl F. H. Henry, the conference chairman, explained the purpose of the consultation, "Ten years after *Newsweek* proclaimed the Year of the Evangelical, the evangelical movement was perceived in terms of Elmer Gantry exploitation and manipulation and confrontational politics. Its cognitive content and its life-ethic has both suffered to the point that the vitality and even survival of the movement may be questioned."[1]

In February 1990, Pat Robertson held a meeting after the National Prayer Breakfast in Washington, D.C. to call for the formation of a Christian antidefamation league. "You've called us fools, so we'll call you bigots! . . . Christians are tired of being stepped on," he told the crowd of about a hundred supporters. "And the time has come to stand up for Christians' rights." In response, one leader observed, "For one of America's strongest, most historic, and sizable faith communities to pass itself off as a beleaguered minority is an insult to real minorities, and an extraordinary testimony to current levels of evangelical paranoia and pessimism."[2]

In April 1990, against the backdrop of Wall Street scandals and the Savings and Loan crisis, an ad hoc group of evangelical business and political leaders hosted the first of two consultations on Christian leadership in business and national life. Their purpose was to explore the perceived crisis in American society and their responsibility to provide spiritual and ethical leadership. Senator Bill Armstrong chaired the proceedings. He told the participants, "We're on a war-time footing." Another speaker issued this challenge: "America has yet to see the consequences of strategic initiatives carried forward by leaders whose business prowess is matched by their faith, vision, and resolve."[3]

In the summer of 1991, the Joshua Project announced a conference in full-page advertisements in evangelical publications. Led by a coalition of fundamentalist activists, the project aimed to "take back the culture." The conference material described its purpose as "to sound the alarm, to instill the vision, and to establish the leadership that will enable us to reclaim the heart of our culture." "America," they acknowledged, "is primarily led, influenced, and instructed by what we have called the 'power bases.' Slowly but surely, through neglect on our part, and an aggressive anti-Christian minority, these power bases have been converted from citadels of justice and mercy to haunts of injustice and cruelty." The conference was canceled for lack of interest.

In September 1991, evangelist Billy Graham, elder statesman of the evangelical movement, addressed two hundred fifty thousand people in New York City's Central Park—his largest American audience ever. Yet even as he spoke, many wondered aloud whether the movement Graham has symbolized for nearly fifty years will be able to sustain its leadership and direction. The New York gathering appeared as the sunset crusade for the man and the movement.

In 1992 the leadership of the National Association of Evangelicals began a reevaluation and strategic planning process in preparation for the retirement of Billy Melvin, who began serving as its executive director in 1967, and for the selection of his successor. Some executive committee members acknowledged that the NAE has not kept pace with the broader changes within evangelicalism, and that its role within the movement needs careful reevaluation.

Ineffective evangelism, a search for identity, playing the victim, a call to arms, withdrawal from engagement, a crisis of leadership—today America's first and once dominant faith community faces serious challenges. In 1848 Marx suggested that "all that is solid melts into air, all that is holy is profaned" under the conditions of modernity.[4] A hundred and fifty years later, the scorching heat of advanced modernity has become the supreme test for evangelical belief and practice. Theologian David Wells laments, "Evangelicalism. . . now appears in full retreat before the clamor of its many special interests. Its essence, like the morning mist, is disappearing in the bright light of modern pluralism."[5]

We evangelicals are acutely aware of our loss of influence in national life. We have demonstrated a variety of cultural responses in our attempt to regain cultural standing. Perplexed by pluralism and outraged at the growing secularity of society, we sometimes vacillate between a majoritarian activism or a victimized passivity, between an anti-modern protest against secular ideas or an uncritical acceptance of the tools of modernity.

This book is an assessment of the state of American evangelicalism. But it is not a dry, removed, and merely academic assessment. Instead it is a call for all evangelicals to recover our true identity, spiritual health, and vitality, by a recommitment to the centrality of the gospel of Jesus Christ.

A PASSION FOR BIBLICAL FIRST THINGS

Who are evangelicals? Symptomatic of the crisis within evangelicalism is the fact that many evangelical leaders and scholars no longer believe evangelicalism can be defined or argue that the term itself needs to be abandoned. Addressing this question has become somewhat of a scholar's cottage industry. Some appeal to evangelicalism's surprising unity of belief in spite of its denominational diversity; others insist on emphasizing its kaleidoscopic diversity.

Four approaches to defining evangelicalism are common. The first is a *confessional or doctrinal definition.* Here evangelicals are defined in terms of what they believe—the core truth commitments that link evangelicalism to other expressions of historic Protestant faith. Such biblical affirmations as that found in 1 Corinthians 15:3 summarize the core of this creed: "Christ died for our sins according to the Scriptures." Yet some evangelical leaders, such as Os Guinness and David Wells, have argued convincingly that evangelicalism as a whole is no longer a movement "defined, directed, or driven by truth." Instead, evangelicalism has become simply a fraternity of religious organizations. This has weakened an identity once based solely on the authority of Scripture and the cross of Jesus Christ.

This shift from theology to sociology has given rise to a second approach, an *institutional definition*. Evangelicalism is defined here particularly by the network of American parachurch institutions that emerged after World War II. These include the World Evangelical Fellowship and umbrella networks, such as the Lausanne Congress on World Evangelization, which itself was born of the vision of the Billy Graham Evangelistic Association.

Since the forties and fifties, evangelical entrepreneurialism has spawned an expanding array of "parallel organizations"— publishing houses, schools, colleges, seminaries, magazines, newspapers, special-interest organizations, law firms, radio stations, television networks, and the like. Yet this vast institutional empire has also given rise to an institutional fragmentation that historian George Marsden compares to a constellation of medieval fiefdoms—superficially friendly but competitive empires that fight for their own expanding turf while professing nominal allegiance to the same distant king.[6]

A third approach defines evangelicalism in terms of *shared experiences*—whether it is the traditional "born-again" experience of regeneration or the more contemporary charismatic experiences. This approach particularly resonates in some parts of the Third World where charismatic evangelicalism is the dominant expression of Protestant belief. In Chile, for example, Pentecostals represent 80 percent of the Protestant population.[7] But Wells suggests that narrowing the essence of evangelicalism to experience alone is itself an accommodation to modernity. Images and feelings replace words and truth.

The fourth approach is the appeal to a *functional definition* of evangelicalism. Such individual religious practices and behavior as church attendance, Bible reading, prayer, and evangelism define this approach. Here pollsters with their statistics and missiologists with their charts take center stage. But in modern society the functional definition frequently masks the declining importance and cultural influence of these behaviors. Nowhere is this more true than in the United States.

For the purpose of this book, I will use a very simple definition of "evangelical." This definition is now being advanced by those who stress unity as well as diversity, and who call for the reformation of the church amid its corruption. It expresses the essential evangelical distinctive: *Evangelicals are those who seek to define themselves and their lives by the demands of the gospel of Jesus Christ. That is, evangelicals are those who have a passion for the first things of the gospel.*

Such a simple affirmation returns our focus to the centrality of the incarnation and the cross and helps us avoid the tendency to reduce evangelicalism to a narrow historical time period or a limited set of institutions. Moreover, "having a passion for biblical first things" emphasizes evangelicalism's historical role of serving as a catalyst for the reformation and revival that unifies the church under the gospel. As Donald Bloesch suggests, the purpose of evangelicalism "is not simply to enhance the spiritual life, but to renew the church by calling it back to its theological and biblical foundations."[8] In this sense then, I speak of myself as an "evangelical" without hesitation.

RELIGION IN THE MIDST OF MODERNITY

To understand the impact of modern life on evangelicalism, we must first examine three common patterns of the relationship between religion and society: diffusion, distinction, and dissociation.

The oldest relationship is characterized by the diffusion of religious beliefs and behaviors throughout society. Wherever this happens, either in traditional Christian societies, such as medieval Europe or colonial America, or in many Third World countries today, all of social life is endowed with a sense of the supernatural, the spiritual, and the sacred.

Sociologist Thomas Luckmann writes that in these societies, "the maintenance and transmission of the sacred universe are based on the social structure in its entirety." Modernity, however, progressively undermines the experience of a sacred universe where faith is diffused throughout. This process of undermining has been called "disenchantment."

It leads to a second pattern—distinction—involving the specialization of religion. Religion is made distinct from other aspects of social life—it is given a separate social location with a specialized body of knowledge. Religious institutions are viewed as just one among many institutions that compete for social and cultural influence. They no longer have an uncontested dominance or respect within the society.

The third relationship, and the one that is the primary feature of high modernity, is the almost complete dissociation of religion from society. Although religion may not decline, it becomes progressively isolated and irrelevant to everyday life.

Two aspects of modernity have contributed to this uniquely modern pattern: pluralization and privatization. Pluralization is the growing diversity of religious options within society. Privatization, in contrast, is the marginalization of religion to the individual, private, and personal sphere of life. Under the conditions of modernity, religion not only faces greater competition, but is simultaneously removed from the central arenas of social life where its influence formerly made a substantive cultural difference.

Religion's loss of cultural influence and respect has led to numerous anti-modern reactions by religious believers in many segments of modern and modernizing societies. In general, these reactions have been of two types. The first reaction attempts to maintain a *consistent anti-modernism*, as seen in the publicized resurgence of Islamic fundamentalism. Cambridge sociologist Ernest Gellner writes, "To say that secularization prevails in Islam is not contentious. It is simply false. Islam is as strong now as it was a century ago. In some ways, it is probably much stronger."[9] Martin Marty has written extensively on the rise of global fundamentalism from within numerous faith traditions. He observes that "Fundamentalism is clearly a force of resentment against 'intellectuals,' 'elites,' 'the media,' and the like, people who are at home with modernization and care little for the presumed traditions."[10] Marty's colleague at the University of Chicago, historian Scott Appleby, adds, "Traditional cultures, with values based in religious teachings, are finding that those values are undermined by the push to modernize societies. . . . Fundamentalists see it as a crisis in which normal procedures must be suspended and they must fight back or their tradition will be lost."[11]

These same tendencies can be seen in contemporary evangelicalism at times, but with an important difference. Evangelicalism more often represents the second type of anti-modernism—an *inconsistent anti-modernism*. Evangelicalism is simultaneously anti-modern and modern, a complex mosaic of both traditional beliefs and modern practices.

From the eighteenth century onward, evangelicalism has shown itself more than a traditional reaffirmation of orthodox belief. It has included explicit accommodations to modernity, such as reliance on technique and technology. Thus contemporary evangelicalism is distinctly different from not only other orthodox belief systems but from its earlier counterparts. This balancing act between an acute anti-modernism and a naive accommodation to modernity shapes the beliefs and behaviors of contemporary evangelicalism. This is what sets evangelicalism apart from Islam and Orthodox Judaism. And this is also what makes evangelicalism particularly prone to the dangers of modernity.

NUMBERS UP, INFLUENCE DOWN

Today evangelicalism faces a quandary. Historically it is the nation's first faith. It has been culturally dominant for most of the nation's history. The number of evangelical churches and evangelicals continues to increase, but our influence within American society is declining. This fact causes confusion among evangelical leaders. On the one hand we are prone to be self-congratulatory when comparing our denominational growth to those of mainline Protestant churches. And yet on the other hand we are fully aware that in spite of a nearly hundred-fifty-year cultural dominance, continuing demographic strength, aggressive political activism, and generous financial contributions, our impact on the culture is weakening. What explains this discrepancy? I believe it can be explained by evangelicals' accommodations to modernity coupled with ineffective cultural strategies.

For years many assumed that modernity would bring about total secularity—the progressive and irreversible disappearance of religion. Yet survey after survey confirms that "by all the normal indicators of religious commitment—the strength of religious institutions, practices, and belief—the United States has resisted the pressures toward secularity."[12] In fact, American religious commitment stands as the greatest exception to the expectation of secularization. The United States remains unique among First World countries in its affirmation of belief and its publicly attestable religious activity. Highly modernized like the First World, the United States is highly religious like the Third World.

A recent Gallup survey found that 80 percent of Americans claim to be Christians—although simultaneously it acknowledged that only 10 to 13 percent are deeply committed.[13] Nonetheless, compared to other First World countries, the religious character of Americans is striking. One only has to compare attendance at weekly religious services in several countries to see the difference—Scandinavia at 5 percent, England at 10 percent, Canada at 25 percent, and the United States at 40 percent.[14] The proportion of Americans who attend church weekly is about the same as that who cast ballots every four years in congressional elections.[15] "Statistically, at least," historian Nathan Hatch claims, "the United States is God's country."[16]

Yet statistics do not always tell the whole story. Modernity has not led to the disappearance of religion, as we noted above. Instead it changes religion's social location and internal character. Modernity rarely challenges religion directly. Spirituality, in fact, can be rather chic in modern society—as long as it stays in its place. Modernity changes the social influence of religion from the public world of business, politics, and education to the private world of self, hobbies, and the family. Religious faith is not challenged as being untrue, but rather assumed to be irrelevant.

Moreover, modernity changes the internal character of religion as the tools of marketing, management, entertainment, and therapy come to compete with traditional spiritual resources. The legitimate benefits of modernity often mask their potential dangers to transcendence, truth, and humanness. This explains why impressive statistical numbers do not automatically reveal the true character of religion in the modern world.

The second reason for evangelicals' weak influence lies in our ineffective cultural strategies, based on our long commitment to populism. Evangelicalism in America is a grassroots, down-to-earth peoples' movement. The movement has historically attracted the dispossessed and the despised. Since the Second Great Awakening, evangelicalism has flourished among the common person. For many years, evangelicals have overlooked the fact that society is shaped by ideas and key institutions. Once evangelicals forfeited leadership of cultural ideas and the leading institutions, an evangelical worldview was itself progressively sidelined in American society.

Culture is shaped, sociologist James Davison Hunter explains, primarily by the influence of elites, not the common person. "While everyone participates in the construction of their own private worlds, the development and articulation of the more elaborate systems of meaning, including the realm of public culture, falls more or less exclusively to the realm of elites. They are the ones who provide the concepts, supply the language, and explicate the logic of public discourse."[17] To a large extent, evangelicals have not been a part of this conversation for over a century.

The ability to shape the consciousness of a society—its taken-for-granted-reality—is the essence of cultural influence. Hunter continues, "The power of culture is not measured by the size of a cultural organization or by the quantity of its output, but by the extent to which a definition of reality is realized in the social world—taken seriously and acted upon by actors in the social world."[18] In modern society religious elites have an existence that is "essentially meaningless to the economic, political, and cultural dynamics of advanced industrial society—a side show to the 'real' issues of the day."[19]

Evangelicals' nineteenth-century cultural and institutional dominance has eroded to the extent that we are rarely perceived as credible participants in national debates. Now at the close of the twentieth century, we find ourselves in a pluralistic religious environment in which we are not at home. "Culturally speaking," Hunter concludes, evangelicals "are strangers in an increasingly strange land."[20]

Deep in the evangelical psyche are conflicting messages of sensed historical entitlement coupled with a feeling of resentment. And so evangelicals are both confused and angry, active and passive. Century-old patterns of social engagement are proving less effective than once hoped. We now must rethink our assumptions about being an evangelical within American society.

A TIME TO RETHINK

We are at a particularly significant time to explore tensions within evangelicalism and to discuss possible ways forward. After almost thirty years of comparative silence and isolation in the public arena, we evangelicals broke out of our cultural isolation in the mid-seventies. Jimmy Carter declared himself "born again" and *Newsweek* proclaimed 1976 as the "Year of the Evangelical."

After a decade and a half of cultural confidence, media exposure, and political activism, evangelicals are beginning to assess the real gains, political and otherwise. Some agree with Robert Fowler, a political scientist from the University of Wisconsin, who stated that there is little to show after the shouting has subsided.[21] But others believe that President Bill Clinton's "liberal agenda" will set off reactions that inject life and new ideas into evangelical cultural engagement.

Nonetheless, evangelical leadership is in a mood of sober reassessment. Evangelical elder-statesman Carl F. H. Henry was asked, "How much optimism do you have that the church in the next decade and beyond will be able to meet the challenges of modernity?" Henry answered bluntly,

> Chuck Colson says in *Against the Night* that if Western cul-
> ture should go down, as well it might, he is not persuaded
> that the churches as we now know them would rise phoenix-
> like above the rubble. I began warning 10 years ago that by
> the 1990s, given the track record of the decisions being made
> by evangelicals, the movement would be in danger of being
> swept away by contemporary culture.[22]

In fact, evangelicalism may be in its most reflective mood since the forties, when a handful of leaders forged a powerful new consensus that has lasted for fifty years. Once again, the evangelical movement is in desperate need of such vision and leadership.

A FAMILY LETTER

This short book is a family letter from one evangelical to evan-
gelical leaders, pastors, and those concerned for the future of the movement. I will describe the serious obstacles that challenge our identity as a movement and compromise our service to Christ's mission. This letter is a warning about the sober choices facing evangelical leaders and institutions in their engagement with modernity. It also is a call to return to our true identity so that we can be a persuasive presence in society.

But first a few words about myself are in order. Research is often a kind of veiled autobiography. Such is the case here. I was raised by evangelical parents who served for thirty-five years as medical missionaries in South Korea. My early discipleship was shaped by the writings of Francis Schaeffer and Inter-Varsity summer camps. I have worked on the staff of a major evangelical parachurch ministry. I have been theologically trained in a growing evangelical seminary. Thus I am well aware of my personal debt to those who have given so much to my life. In short, I am not only an evangelical, but a product of American evangelicalism.

Moreover, like certain evangelical scholars but unlike a good many others, though I am concerned about the state of evangelicalism and its accommodation to modernity, I do not write as a "disenchanted believer," but as one who continues to take his religious commitments and evangelical identity seriously. I do not write as an outsider or with a supposed academic detachment. Instead I write this book with a sense of personal burden. For evangelicalism has shaped both my own identity and my own sense of calling. Its unfolding story is about both my heritage and my obligation to my heirs.

QUESTIONS FOR REFLECTION AND DISCUSSION

1. How do you define "evangelical"? Do you think this term or concept is worth keeping? (see pages 14–16)

2. In what ways is evangelicalism a "complex mosaic of traditional beliefs and modern practices"? (see page 18)

3. How do you explain the fact that evangelical numbers are up but our social influence is down? (see pages 18–21)

2

YESTERDAY'S MAN

"In each of us, in varying proportions, there is part of yesterday's man; it is yesterday's man who inevitably predominates in us, since the present amounts to little compared with the long past in the course of which we were formed and from which we result. Yet we do not sense this man of the past, because he is inveterate in us; he makes up the unconscious part of ourselves."

—Pierre Bourdieu

AMERICANA AT ITS BEST

AT THE FIFTIETH ANNIVERSARY of the National Association of Evangelicals held in Chicago, Illinois in March of 1992, Jay Kesler, president of Taylor University and former president of Youth for Christ, gave the opening plenary address entitled, "Why I Believe in the Evangelical Church and Its Future." President George Bush had spoken to the convention earlier in the day and Billy Graham was scheduled to speak the following evening. The mood was celebratory; the audience was composed of evangelical denominational and parachurch leaders.

Kesler's address was folksy and filled with stories, asides, and anecdotes. He made four points in his speech. He said that he believes in the evangelical church and its future because: it is the only institution in our culture dealing with ultimate issues; it provides perspective and dignity to humans; it provides a moral and ethical compass in the midst of relativism; it is a place where he can find community, healing, and love. But perhaps more importantly, Kesler spoke symbolically. The subtext of his message could be found in his choice of illustrations. These shorthand rhetorical devices traced the deeper roots of the evangelical identity. Some examples follow.

About the president Kesler said, "Amazing thing to think, isn't it, that the president of the United States comes to address the National Association of Evangelicals. I can remember a day when that sort of thing would be political anathema. . . ." Here Kesler spoke to the ambivalence evangelicals feel in American society, a vacillation between majoritarian confidence and minoritarian insecurity.

About pluralism Kesler said,

> I sort of resent it when people treat me like I'm part of some subculture, as if they want to take me and bronze me and sell me on the Pennsylvania Turnpike as a souvenir, some little subculture. . . . I feel this new commitment to civility that's part of being a pluralistic culture, sort of "live and let live." It doesn't matter what you believe. We're all, after all, products of our environment. We just happen to be what we are because we grew up in a certain part of town, or have a certain color of skin. We don't really think anything or believe anything. You can send people from PBS down to see us make dulcimers or something. And frankly, I resent this.

Kesler rightly identified evangelicals' resentment over losing our cultural dominance in American life. The cultural elite have reduced the movement to a curious subculture—the subject of a public television special on folk religions and folk art.

Other topics in his speech were the Scopes Monkey trial, the collapse of Marxism, the priority of world missions, crime in the cities, the dangers of relativism, the inerrancy of Scripture, the Wesley revivals, the nineteenth-century reform movements, little-town America, and family values.

Kesler ended his speech by referring to the Rose Bowl Parade and the deep ties it evidenced between American patriotism and evangelical faith. He said,

> The Rose Bowl Parade is amazing, a wonderful time—Americana at its best. Float goes by and "General Motors spent three quarters of a million dollars on this float." "Ooh, ahh!" And you start hearing applause off in the distance. There's only one sustained applause at the Rose Parade. And it's not for a million dollar float, it's for a little group of people in funny blue suits with little squashed trumpets, carrying the Christian and American flags, playing "Onward Christian Soldiers."
>
> There isn't a man in the world who's been in the service, or who's been in the midst of a hurricane or tornado or national disaster, or been down on his luck in some city, who doesn't recognize pure religion, undefiled. And secular man gives sustained applause at the Rose Parade every year for the real thing.

Kesler noted correctly that to understand America one must appreciate the deep resonance of the Christian faith within the nation. But the reverse is also true. Evangelicalism has much of America within it. In short, I will argue in this chapter that "yesterday's man" is more Americana-cum-debased-nineteenth-century-evangelicalism than the real thing. Modern American evangelicals have largely abandoned our historical connection to pre-American evangelicals—to the patristic fathers, the reformers, the Puritan divines, and others. American evangelicals have an American psyche. And so it is the logic of this interior history that explains the rhetorical power of Kesler's speech that evening in Chicago. His message resonated with the American evangelical sense of self.

CONTOURS OF AN EVANGELICAL IDENTITY

American evangelical history illustrates numerous stances toward culture engagement. As George Marsden notes, "On the issues of culture and politics generalizations about evangelicalism are particularly hazardous."[1] Behind many of these practices lie a shared unconscious history. This history, framing as it does much of the evangelical self-understanding and disposition toward culture, regrettably has come to have a greater relationship to evangelical practice than do theological beliefs or worldviews. This history explains the paradoxes of evangelical cultural practice but also poses a significant challenge to the recovery of a genuine evangelicalism.

Knowing one's past is integral to a sense of identity—the sureness of "I was" is needed for the sureness of "I am." A moving account of this notion is given in John Steinbeck's classic *The Grapes of Wrath*. As the uprooted Okies prepare for their trip to California—the land of the uprooted—they face painful decisions as to what they can take and what must be left behind. Steinbeck writes,

> In the little houses the tenant people sifted their belongings and the belongings of their fathers and of their grandfathers. Picked over their possessions for the journey to the west. The men were ruthless because the past had been spoiled, but the women knew how the past would cry to them in the coming days. . . . The women sat among the doomed things, turning them over and looking past them and back. . . . How can we live without our lives? How will we know it's us without our past? No. Leave it. Burn it. They sat and looked at it and burned it into their memories.[2]

Historian Anthony Brandt observes that a real appreciation of the past "requires something more than knowing how people used to make candles or what kinds of beds they slept in. It requires a sense of the persistence of the past: the manifold ways in which it penetrates our lives."[3] Marx correctly noted, "Men make their own history, but they do not make it just as they please; they do not make it under circumstances chosen by themselves, but under circumstances directly encountered, given, and transmitted from the past."[4] French theorist Pierre Bourdieu adds, "It is yesterday's man who inevitably predominates us."[5] For American evangelicalism this means that certain historical experiences and mythical themes have been interwoven into our psyche, into our sense of self. Five historical moments are particularly salient to the evangelical identity.

A City on a Hill (1630–1800)

"Where are you coming from?" "The founder's vision. . ." "My roots. . ." We use these and other phrases in everyday life to point out the importance of beginnings or places of origin. Anthropologists have found that myths of origin, whether understood in religious or purely secular terms, play a powerful role in giving meaning to existence. For example Mircea Eliade writes in *Myth and Reality*,

> Myth narrates a sacred history; it relates an event that took place in primordial time, the fabled time of the "beginnings." In other words, myth tells how a reality came into existence, be it the whole of reality, the Cosmos, or only a fragment of reality—an island, a species of plant, a particular kind of human behavior, an institution. Myth, then, is always an account of a "creation"; it relates how something was produced, began to be.[6]

American evangelical identity is closely tied to America's myth of origin. America was, in Seymour Martin Lipset's phrase, the world's "first new nation." It was founded by a profoundly religious people, many of whom came to America explicitly seeking religious freedom.

The experiences of these first settlers—their beliefs and vision—continue to resonate powerfully in American public rhetoric. In the 1988 presidential campaign, both Michael Dukakis and George Bush related their political vision to John Winthrop's sermon on the *Arabella*. Dukakis quoted from a passage early in the sermon, "Every man might have need of other, and from hence they might be knit more nearly together in the bond of brotherly affection." Bush reminded Americans of the sermon's famous ending, "We must consider that we shall be as a city upon a hill. . . If we shall deal falsely with our God in this work. . . we shall be made a story and a by-word through the world."[7]

For most American evangelicals, these words are not understood as political posturing, but as an identification with the true American vision. They see themselves as the spiritual heirs of those sea-weary Puritans who landed at Massachusetts Bay. Winthrop's sermon is an exhortation directed to them. To understand contemporary American evangelicals, we must acknowledge the contribution of the early Puritans and determine how evangelicals view the Puritans as the basis for their sense of communal legitimation and national entitlement. In short, some evangelicals suggest that America was founded by evangelicals, for evangelicals.

The original colonists were more diverse than many realize, separated from each other by both geography and heritage. They represented a wide variety of religious traditions—from the Puritans in New England to the members of the Church of England in Virginia's tidewater region to Catholics in Maryland and Florida. Yet the New England colonies and the English Puritan legacy—tempered by the Enlightenment—played a special role in shaping the formation of the new nation. Not only did the Puritan notion of covenant contribute structurally to the formation of the Constitution, but the Puritan sense of divine mission provided a mythic rationale for the new nation.

Whether America was in fact founded as a "Christian nation" is a point of some dispute. Both sides of the debate are prone to overstatement. Some would suggest that there was almost no Christian ethos operating at the time of the nation's founding. Others, in contrast, would almost turn committed Deists into devout evangelicals. Facts, quotes, and examples are marshaled on both sides.

A residual Christian worldview did play a dominant role in the framers' minds. Historian Sidney Ahlstrom concludes that

"Puritanism provided the moral and religious background of fully 75 percent of the people who declared their independence in 1776."[8] Whether each individual had a genuine faith commitment or not, we must acknowledge that eighteenth-century Deism was far closer to a biblical view of reality than is modern secularism.

Despite the nation's Puritan ethos, the framers clearly did not intend to create a nation where the Christian faith had a special status or privilege. This is the view, however, that many evangelicals continue to advocate. And so the emotionally loaded term "Christian America" persists in our views of history, is widely promoted in Christian school curriculum, is assumed normative by evangelical special-interest groups, and is appealed to by "Christian" political candidates. The logic of this argument is that the Christian influence in the nation's founding suggests the founders' intention to establish a Christian nation, which now justifies a contemporary evangelical appeal to a sense of historical entitlement. Such views, they would argue, are consistent with our national "myth of origin."

Most scholars would disagree with this type of argument. The nation's roots were primarily (though not exclusively) Christian, and the Christian faith has been the prominent faith throughout America history. But it is neither factually accurate nor constitutionally justified to assert any special, official status given to the Christian faith. Yet evangelical public discourse has frequently suggested otherwise.[9]

Too often evangelicals dangerously confuse Americanism with evangelicalism. As early as 1835, Alexis de Tocqueville noted, "It must never be forgotten that religion gave birth to Anglo-American society. In the United States, religion is therefore mingled with all the habits of the nation and all the feelings of patriotism, whence it derives a peculiar force."[10] An uncritical blending of identities may lead us to forget Whose we really are and what kingdom claims our ultimate loyalty and citizenship. Yet notions of a Christian America continue to mold much of evangelicalism.

We the People (1800–1880)

Equally as important as the Puritan period in shaping the evangelical identity are the events surrounding the Second Great Awakening (1800–1830). No single period in American history provides more insights into the factors that gave rise to contemporary evangelicalism.

During this period a frontier populism replaced New England Puritanism. This populism remains as one of the deepest impulses in American religious life. Hatch writes, "The rise of evangelical Christianity in the early republic is, in some measure, a story of the success of common people in shaping the culture after their own priorities rather than the priorities outlined by gentlemen such as the framers of the Constitution."[11] Religious populism was furthered by institutional changes stemming from the disestablishment of religion, all of which reinforced the ideological glorification of the "common man" of the Jacksonian era.

The institutional change came with the adoption of the First Amendment religious liberty clauses in 1791. Hereafter the Constitution required an institutional separation of church and state, no longer allowing "religion to use the government's sword and purse to become the coercing Church."[12] This was the first such structural disestablishment of religion in the Western political experience. It was a radical departure from historical precedence; clearly the framers knew this significance. Six years after the Bill of Rights was ratified (1791), the Senate passed a treaty with Tripoli that George Washington initiated and President John Adams signed, which read:

> As the government of the United States of America is not in any sense founded on the Christian Religion—as it has in itself no character of enmity against the laws, religion or tranquillity of Muslims. . . it is declared by the parties that no pretext arising from religious opinion shall ever produce an interruption of the harmony existing between the two countries.[13]

Though Protestantism continued as the dominant belief of Americans, hereafter all religious traditions and denominations were put squarely within the spirit of American market entrepreneurialism, each competing for its own adherents. Those groups that best responded to the needs of the common person and demands of an expanding nation were rewarded. Northeastern religious elites lost constituents as Americans rushed to the Western frontier. But even more telling, they lost legitimacy in a religious climate that not only glorified the common but promoted emotional experience over arid intellectualism.

Four characteristics of this period continue to shape the modern evangelical identity: anti-elitism, anti-intellectualism, technical rationality, and moral reform.

The first aspect of this populist Christian faith involved a *revolt against elites* in all aspects of American culture. In 1828 the Eastern intellectual political legacy of the framers, symbolized by presidential candidate John Quincy Adams, was abandoned for Andrew Jackson—the "natural man from the West." The formerly respected professions of law, medicine, and the clergy came under frequent attack. Once out of the bottle, the "spirit of 1776" became a challenge to all protected elites and long-revered traditions.

This anti-elitism had two additional consequences. First, the antagonism against elites frequently led to a suspicion of them and the rise of conspiracy theories. During this period the nation's troubles were variously described as caused by the politicians and clergy who serve special interests, the Catholic church, Masons, liquor dealers, or slave power. These were the supposed dangers plotting against the liberties of the people.

During this period nativism spawned the Know-Nothing party. It was based on the slogan, "Americans must rule America." By "Americans" they meant only WASP Americans. The political power of nativism and anti-Catholic feeling was witnessed in 1856 when former President Millard Fillmore ran as the American Party presidential candidate and attracted 20 percent of the popular vote.

The second consequence of this rejection of traditional elites was the emergence of new leaders whose power was not based on position or education but on coarse, backwoods appeal. The Second Great Awakening was a movement centered around charismatic leaders who used "democratic persuasion to reconstruct the foundations of religious authority."[14] Under the guise of a protest against elites, in fact, a new class of elites emerged. Those who captured the imagination of the common person were rewarded with the largest followings.

A second characteristic of these evangelical forebears involved a *philosophically reinforced anti-intellectualism*. This anti-intellectualism was accentuated by class antagonism, but it also developed both a popular and philosophical rationale. Although it did not involve a wholesale repudiation of the mind, it did advocate an immediacy to knowledge that rejected the necessity for formal education. People had a heightened confidence in an individual's ability, with the Bible as the source, to speak authoritatively about all areas of life.

Motivated by class resentment and supported by common-sense philosophy, anti-intellectualism became a dominant feature of American evangelical Protestantism. Moreover, between the years 1800 and 1850, the church consciously withdrew from the intellectual life of the nation. "By 1853," wrote historian Richard Hofstadter, "an outstanding clergyman complained that there was 'an impression, somewhat general, that an intellectual clergyman is deficient in piety, and that an eminently pious minister is deficient in intellect.' "[15]

The third characteristic of evangelicalism was the *use of technique*. The major difference between the First Great Awakening under such Puritans as George Whitefield and the Second Great Awakening under such leaders as Charles Finney was that revivals were no longer based on God's sovereign work but on the application of humanly engineered techniques—nightly meetings, vernacular preaching, gospel choruses, exhortations by women, the "anxious bench," mass publicity, and the like. Finney was so confident in these new techniques that he wrote,

"Perhaps it is not too much to say, that it is impossible for God himself to bring about reformation but by new measures."[16]

Moreover, because of evangelical anti-intellectualism, theological truth was judged finally by its results in the marketplace. Numbers came to trump truth. Ministers were evaluated by their ability to "get results"—specifically the saving of souls in measurable amounts. The "whole counsel of God" was reduced to the "how-to's" of human reason—a shift in emphasis from "spiritual faithfulness" to "spiritual fruit." In 1817 Congregationalist Thomas Andros wrote a biting critique of these tendencies: "They measure the progress of religion by the numbers, who flock to their standard; not by the prevalence of faith, and piety, justice, charity, and the public virtues in society in general."[17]

The fourth characteristic that shaped evangelicalism during this period was *grassroots moral advocacy*. One might have thought that the "soul-winning" priority of nineteenth-century evangelicals would have tended to undermine an equal concern for social engagement. But this was not so, because of two aspects of evangelical theology that dominated this period: the doctrine of Christian perfection and postmillennialism.

The doctrine of Christian perfection emphasized such a depth of personal transformation that a high level of personal holiness was expected. The perfection doctrine, in its variety of forms, created a powerful imperative for ethical earnestness based on the believer's entire consecration to God's will. Doctrinal belief was not divorced from a practical expression in life. To be indifferent to social evils was thought to be as unfaithful as thinking that social evils could be resolved by human effort alone.

Yet the reform initiatives only began in earnest when they were combined with the doctrine of postmillennialism. This is the view that history is the progressive unfolding of Christian triumph over evil and that Christ's return depends on Christian activity that shapes a new world characterized by prosperity, peace, and righteousness. Historian Timothy Smith argues that "revivalism and perfectionism became socially volatile only when combined with the doctrine of Christ's imminent conquest of the earth."[18] Throughout the nineteenth century, evangelicals were actively involved in promoting social change, from the abolition of slavery to the temperance movement. Social reform and evangelistic fervor were a unified mission.

Thus the modern American evangelical identity is rooted in a one-hundred-fifty-year-old history. Few evangelicals today know the names of Lorenzo Dow, Charles Finney, or Alexander Campbell, but the stamp of their historical legacy on evangelical attitudes is pervasive. Nathan Hatch concludes that the driving force behind American Christianity is not the quality of its organizations, the status of its clergy, or the vitality of its intellectual life. The central factor is its populism.

These attitudes still shape our approach toward cultural engagement—evangelicals continue to be predisposed to a suspicion of elites, an anti-intellectual confidence in mass opinion, and an uncritical reliance on technologies appropriate to mass mobilization. Our unthinking populism stands today as the single greatest roadblock to effective cultural engagement.

Loss of Cultural Dominance (1880–1930)

As the nineteenth century ended, evangelicals continued to hold an apparent cultural dominance in spite of a decreasing spiritual vitality. But within a generation evangelicals had lost their intellectual prestige and cultural power. Gaius Glenn Atkins, who lived through this period of change, wrote of the years after 1890 that "no other four decades, or forty decades either, in the history of Christian thought had seen so many and such momentous changes in fundamental religious attitudes."[19] This loss of cultural dominance was due to sweeping economic, social, and intellectual changes in the nation that evangelicals were unprepared to handle. These challenges also revealed weaknesses within evangelicalism.

American culture after the turmoil of the Civil War has been described as a "society without a core." A common postwar reaction was to focus on the personal concerns of family, neighborhood, and community. Few Americans were prepared for the rapid social changes of the late nineteenth century—the movement from rural areas to the urban centers, the shift from an agricultural economy to an industrial economy, or the massive influx of immigrants after 1880. The city, the machine, the corporation, and the foreigner were the symbols of a changing America in the late nineteenth century.

But a pincer movement caused the collapse of the Protestant hegemony. First, religious belief was hollowed out by a gradual acceptance of consumer values. Second, religious institutions were assaulted by academic challenges to the authority of Scripture. The collapse was also two-staged—first it was intellectual, then it was popular. The shifts in the 1870s and 1880s became apparent among intellectuals and artists in the 1920s and 1930s. But it was only in the turbulent 1960s that they became apparent in the wider culture. Early forms of relativism, such as notions that all truths are relative to their own historical age, entered the social disciplines in the university in the 1880s and were largely taken-for-granted by the 1920s. By 1914 pragmatism, Darwinism, legal realism, the new history, and economic determinism were the popular doctrines.

Within popular religious belief, faith was not so much disavowed as simply abandoned. During the interwar years (1920–1930) sociologists Robert and Helen Lynd conducted their famous Middletown study and found that religion in America had shifted from "a set of beliefs to a social occasion."[20] By the end of the thirties a secular vocabulary had replaced a theological vocabulary when issues of importance were discussed.

The first aspect of this collapse was the weakening of faith from within—the acceptance of consumerism and its parallel language of self-fulfillment. This is the story of city values replacing small-town values. Although the myth of the West is vintage Americana of this period, historian David Potter notes that more Americans changed their status during this time by moving to the city than to the frontier.[21]

SET OF BELIEFS   THEOLOGICAL VOCAB

SOCIAL OCCASION   SECULAR VOCAB

One historian writes that city values were basically con-sumer values: "Consumption emerged as the hidden purpose of cities. . . . In the end, the paradoxes of Vanity Fair, its specta-cles of mystery in street and park, in home and store, in regions fragmented and set against each other, arose from the increas-ingly arcane practices of buying and selling."[22] Fueled by the advent of mass advertising, the society shifted from being ori-ented from production toward consumption, from self-denial to self-fulfillment.

Many Americans decried the loss of small-town America and its small-town values. But ironically, Jackson Lears suggests that in the late nineteenth century those who were most anti-modern in their outlook began to resort to the "therapeutic ideal of self-fulfillment," consequently hastening the acceptance of the twentieth-century culture of consumption.[23]

This was specifically true of the religious community. Busi-ness values merged with religious values. Moody was a man of his time. He promoted religion with all the organization of Andrew Carnegie and all the hype of P. T. Barnum. Lyman Abbott wrote of Moody, "he looked like a business man; he dressed like a business man; he took the meeting in hand as a business man would; he spoke in a business man's fashion."[24]

Rollo Ogden wrote about the same trends in the Nation in 1886, "Indeed, so far has the church caught the spirit of the age," "so far has it become a business enterprise, that the chief test of ministerial success is now the ability to 'build up' a church. Exec-utive, managerial abilities are now more in demand than those which used to be considered the highest in a clergyman."[25]

This shift to consumer values helped create a hollowness in past certainties. Historians refer to this period as undergoing a "crisis of cultural authority"—the beliefs of the past were losing their binding power in the face of early modernity. Lears writes, "The religious sanction for bourgeois morality, the supernatural framework which gave life meaning and purpose, seemed to be dissolving in a haze of enlightened platitudes."[26] Bourgeois moral-ity became an end in itself, divorced from the convictions and vitality of genuine religious conversion. Children were taught from *The McGuffey Reader*, college students attended classes in moral philosophy—but these moral convictions had an increasingly second-hand feel. Lears concludes, "Educated Americans, facing dilemmas they could scarcely define, lacked the religious certainty of their grandparents. Ancestral theological armor lay in disuse, corroded by secularization."[27]

During this same period, while the evangelical hegemony was collapsing all around them, many evangelicals became focused on a narrow agenda—alcohol. Frequently when foundational issues are besieged, symbolic issues begin to take precedence. So it was during the first years of the twentieth century. James Reichley writes:

FOUNDATIONAL
SYMBOLIC

> Liquor, along with its attendant institutions, the saloon and beer hall, seem to have summed up and symbolized many of the cultural and social tendencies that appeared to be challenging the evangelical's view of life: the increased openness to sensual pleasure, the growing intellectual authority of scientific rationalism, the decline of the work ethic, the concentration of population in large cities, and the increasing presence in eastern and midwestern cities of non-English-speaking immigrants, mostly Catholics or Jews from southern and eastern Europe.[28]

Finally, it was during this period that evangelicals all but abandoned their social and cultural concern. In part, this reversal was an overreaction to the Social Gospel movement, but it was also a way to dismiss a growing awareness of a looming cultural defeat. A narrowed concern for personal piety and individual conversion replaced the confident cultural rhetoric of the previous generation. Marsden writes:

> In retrospect, we can see that the decade preceding America's entry into the Great War was the end of an era for the American evangelical establishment. Throughout the nineteenth century there had seemed to be a reasonable hope for establishing the foundations of something like a 'Christian

America.' With the knowledge of what has happened since, it is apparent that this ideal was illusory and that the evangelical consensus itself was irreparably damaged.[29]

William Jennings Bryan, sometimes called the "George Custer of fundamentalism," won a celebrated courtroom victory at the Scopes Trial in 1925. But the courtroom spectacle was simultaneously a nationwide cultural defeat for fundamentalists. They became the target of intense intellectual and journalistic assault. Evangelicals came to be viewed as narrow-minded, dogmatic, authoritarian, superstitious, simplistic bumpkins, and a Neanderthal subculture.

The cultural tide had changed and no jury decision could hold back its advancing secularizing waves. Under increasing pressure, evangelicals reacted by creating their own equivalent of the urban ghetto. "Fundamentalists, excluded from the community of modern theological and scientific orthodoxy, eventually were forced to establish their own theological and scientific subculture in which their own ideas of orthodoxy were preserved."[30]

An evangelical worldview had weakened intellectually and institutionally. But it was almost fifty years later until evangelicals realized the full extent of the erosion of a Christian system of morality. Contemporary American evangelicals carry the memory of this traumatic cultural paradigm shift.

From Culture to Subculture (1930–1970)

With the creation of an evangelical subculture, mainstream denominations progressively lost influence as monolithic, homogeneous structures. But evangelicalism itself became a structurally fragmented federation of special-interest groups centered around the personal ministries of charismatic leaders. Evangelicals' uniting vision in this period was a common commitment to the priority of evangelism and world missions. Robert Wuthnow states that evangelicals of this period thought that whereas "faith had formerly been weakened by differences over nonessentials; now, if only Christ could be preached, rather than denominational distinctives or ethical programs, great strength could be realized."[31]

Yet narrowing the focus of religious practice to evangelism removed evangelical impetus for social engagement. White evangelical churches were strangely silent during the civil rights movement. Instead of activism, evangelicals appealed to individual conversion as the only lasting means of social change. "If values were the key to a healthy society and if personal renewal were the key to healthy values, then there was really no conflict between an emphasis on individual faith and a concern for the common good."[32]

Yet ironically just as evangelicals created separate institutions for evangelistic outreach, they became increasingly out of touch with American society. It became easier and easier for evangelicals to live from the womb to the tomb in an insulated evangelical ghetto—attending Christian schools and evangelical colleges, reading evangelical magazines, listening to religious radio, watching Christian television programming, and so on. Thus by sequestrating themselves into a cognitive enclave, evangelicals became increasingly parochial in outlook. Moreover, evangelical leadership was frequently limited to those who graduated from evangelical institutions, such as Wheaton College or Moody Bible Institute. Consequently evangelical practice reinforced the social fragmentation that modernity fosters.

Evangelical Identity Exposed (1970–Present)

So when evangelicals reemerged into the national spotlight in the mid-seventies, they emerged with the patterns of thought characterized by decades of religious privatization and social isolation. This isolation had two consequences.

First, the scope of concern was narrowed to the private world of family and home. The religious right became politically mobilized because they felt that Supreme Court decisions in the sixties (prayer in schools) and seventies (abortion rights) intruded on their private world. Hunter writes,

Protestants long ago conceded control over the affairs of state and economy, education, and other institutional areas, but the family, sexuality, and the private sphere generally—the wellspring of moral discipline in society—have remained heavily under their influence. The private sphere, and the family in particular, may prove to be the final battleground in conservative Protestantism's century-long battle with modernity.[33]

Evangelical special-purpose groups continue to have their broadest appeal when directed to family issues—such as in James Dobson's Focus on the Family and Beverly LaHaye's Concerned Women for America. The religious right is frequently accused of "single-issue politics." But this tendency is understandable because their religious convictions are perceived to be most relevant to those issues. Single-issue politics is simply the political fallout of a privatized faith.

The second consequence of a privatized faith was the loss of a publicly accessible language in which to enter the public debate in an increasingly secular and pluralistic society. Much of evangelicals' political discourse of the eighties was little more than impassioned rhetoric that persuaded no one.

Just as a publicly accessible discourse was absent in the arena of hard-ball politics and public policy debates, evangelical organizations soon became aware of difficulties in communicating the basic tenets of the faith. The Navigators issued a special report in 1987 that stated, "the influence of secularization in our society has resulted in the gospel message being perceived as an irrelevant message to many in the United States. One major reason is that secularization has affected people's world views and these divergent world views have affected communication between Christians and non-Christians. . . . Therefore, when a Christian attempts to communicate the gospel in a sub-culture that is not his own, language meanings can become a barrier."[34]

Thus for forty years, evangelicals had created a powerful, national network of institutional supports. What began as an attempt to maintain the boundaries of orthodoxy, a beachhead from which to engage the broader society, degenerated into its own lifestyle enclave. Moreover, the size of this enclave made it a viable market niche, adding an economic rationale to this fortress mentality. Evangelicals began to act like a political interest group concerned with a narrow agenda rather than those who advocate a broader social vision for all Americans.

THIS PRESENT PSYCHE

The reassertion of evangelicals into public prominence during the mid-seventies cannot be understood in isolation from these historically rooted dispositions. The paradoxes and tensions evidenced in evangelical public behavior result from the historical, rather than theological, consistency of our identity. Yet this unconscious memory continues to shape the behavior of Protestant orthodoxy just as powerfully as the experience of the Holocaust continues to shape the Jewish community.

Nowhere is this seen more clearly than in the writings of Frank Peretti. Better than any contemporary writer, Peretti describes with psychoanalytical clarity a world that reveals the mythic themes that continue to shape the evangelical psyche. This populist storyteller has achieved enormous and unexpected fame for two Christian bestsellers, *This Present Darkness* (1986) and *Piercing the Darkness* (1989). Together the books have sold over 3 million copies since their release.

In its first year *This Present Darkness* sold only four thousand copies. By 1988 the numbers rose to twenty-four thousand. Then in 1988, pop Christian singer Amy Grant began recommending the book at her concerts. Peretti became a household name in evangelical circles overnight. His sequel, *Piercing the Darkness*, was published with an unprecedented first printing of 1.5 million copies. A major motion picture contract is in the works with Howard Kazanjian—a Steven Lucas collaborator. Peretti's latest book, *Prophet*, was released in the spring of 1992.

Though Peretti is marketed with hyperbolic adulation, these books are no better than pulp fiction. Yet he is compared shamelessly to such great Christian writers as George Macdonald, C. S. Lewis, and J. R. Tolkien. A British reviewer states, "The regrettable truth is that Peretti's novels are pastiche compilations from the gigantic out-pouring of American trash literature over the last half-century or so—costumed hero comics, thrillers and war stories. They are badly written and repetitive—'puffed wheat' literature in which the tiny grains of content are inflated to five hundred or more sides."[35] Calvin Miller, a pastor and respected fiction writer states, "The best description of *This Present Darkness* I've heard is 'Stephen King meets David Hunt.' "

Nonetheless Peretti represents an evangelical publishing phenomena. In the last four years he has appeared seven times in the Christian Booksellers Association annual listing of the bestselling books with an average ranking of 2.2 (1 being the highest). James Dobson had eleven listings with an average ranking of 6.45; Charles Swindoll had seven listings with an average of 7.1.

In 1992, Peretti was a keynote speaker at the Christian Booksellers Association convention, and in the 1993 *Christianity Today* Reader's Poll *Prophet* was ranked number two. More significantly, when *Christianity Today* readers were asked "What is your favorite novel of all time?" *This Present Darkness* ranked fourth behind Dostoevsky's *The Brother's Karamazov* and *Piercing the Darkness* ranked eighth behind C. S. Lewis' *Perelandra*.[36]

Why do *This Present Darkness* and *Piercing the Darkness* appeal so powerfully to the American evangelical community? Because they tell a story that describes how evangelicals feel at the close of the twentieth century. They resonate with our identity. To illustrate, some examples from these books follow.

> The pretty little saints in the town were. . . obscure, don't you see, far from help, far from the mainstream, alone amid the rolling farmlands, unknown. It was the perfect place to begin the process.[37]

From here the town looked so typically American—small, innocent, and harmless, like the background for every Norman Rockwell painting.[38]

It could have begun in any town. Bacon's Corner was nothing special, just one of those little farming towns far from the interstate, nothing more than a hollow dot on the AAA road map, with exit signs that offered gas, no lodging, maybe a little food if the place was open, and little more. But it began in Bacon's Corner.[39]

The Bacon's Corner Elementary School reeked of demons. . . . The playground was full of kids, about two hundred, running, playing, and squealing before the first bell signaled the start of classes. Then they would gather in all those classrooms where the spirits would be busy, more than ever before.[40]

He leaned forward and lowered his voice. "Everything Langstreet does is a deep, dark secret! The Inner Circle, Bernice. No one is even supposed to know about these so-called consultations, no one but the privileged, the elite, the powerful, the many special patrons that go to her."[41] "Bernice, we are dealing with a conspiracy of spirit entities."[42]

The little people—the Christians—get into legal tangles because of the state, or the ACFA, or some other rabid, Christian-eating secularist organization decides to pick on them, and those people always have all the power, connections, and finances they need to win any battle they want in a court of law. Not so with Christians.[43]

There's still a Remnant of saints somewhere in this town. There is always a Remnant.[44]

His strength is not in his sword, but in the saints of God. Somewhere somebody is praying.[45] Tal took a quick survey of his prayer cover he had gathered. It had to be enough for tonight's plan to work.[46]

Peretti tells a story of small town America, of disenfranchised evangelicals who face Satanic conspiracies masked behind multinational businessmen, university professors, public school administrators, welfare social workers, ACLU lawyers, ecological fanatics, and New Age gurus. In spite of their apparent intellectual and cultural impotence, these beleaguered believers shape the course of history through their "prayer cover" that empowers God's angels against Satan's demons. Peretti's bestsellers are book-length illustrations of evangelicals' compensation for the loss of cultural influence. They are pious rationalizations of past failures and potentially self-fulfilling prophecies.

Thus much of what we think is an expression of a biblical evangelical identity is actually shaped by unique American influences. Isolated from historical precedents and narrowed by our ethnocentric blinders, the power of the gospel is perverted by a Yankee provincialism.

Peretti's two novels illustrate how difficult it will be for American evangelicals to consider changing our identity. The task of returning to a biblical identity requires that we first question much of what is taken for granted within evangelicalism. Majoritarian politics, grassroots populism, conspiracy theories, reliance on technique, attitudes of resentment, loss of public commitment, and absence of persuasion are all patterns seen in the recent evangelical resurgence.

A sober revaluation is in order. History may have shaped our dispositions, but it is up to us to choose our future direction. It is time for us to repent of unfaithfulness. We must rethink how we should resist the temptations of our present cultural moment as we play our part in the unfolding story of God's kingdom.

QUESTIONS FOR REFLECTION AND DISCUSSION

1. How does history shape our identity? What are the dangers of not knowing one's identity?

2. Which of the five historical periods has most shaped your own sense of what it means to be an evangelical?

3. What Christian books have you read recently that reinforce the historical attitudes discussed in this chapter?

3

THE CRISES OF EVANGELICALISM

"For a century or so, evangelicals defined the culture; they were not, as were, say Orthodox Jews, a minority. As a consequence, there has never been systematic reflection on the part of the evangelical community on how they can preserve their faith, their way of life, and their community, indeed, their very identity as a religious people, in an environment that might be hostile."
—James Davison Hunter

A LEADER'S VIEW

THIS CHAPTER EXAMINES the state of evangelicalism through the perspectives of twenty-five leaders and gatekeepers within the evangelical movement. They represent a spectrum of views within the broad mainstream movement symbolized by the National Association of Evangelicals and *Christianity Today*—the movement that grew in the United States after World War II. As such, the interviews provide insights about evangelicalism at a key moment of transition.

These interviews were conducted to gain a "leader's view" of the state of evangelicalism firsthand. The picture painted by these interviews is not intended to be statistically significant. Nor does it provide a profile of the wider body of people who make up the 16 percent of Americans who identify themselves as "evangelical." But the interviews are significant because they reveal trends and themes among the group who leads evangelicals and evangelical institutions. Eight major themes emerged from these discussions, and are summarized below.

WHO, WHAT, WHEN, WHERE, AND WHY

I conducted these interviews during the spring and summer of 1992 with representative evangelicals from four major religious and theological traditions: Anabaptist, Baptist, Holiness-Pentecostal, and Reformational-Confessional. Respondents were chosen for representing nine institutional categories and seven geographical regions. The institutions represented were associations, churches, management consultants, denominations, colleges, foundations, parachurch agencies, publishing houses, and seminaries. The broad regions sampled were Atlanta, Boston, Chicago, Colorado Springs, Los Angeles, Orlando, and Washington, D.C.

The interviews were not only with the official "leaders" of evangelicalism, however arbitrarily they might be identified, but with evangelical "gatekeepers." These are individuals whose resources (education, wealth, relationships, or social status) and/or responsibilities give them privileged access to the institutions that shape the meaning and direction of evangelicalism. Some of these individuals may not be as well known as others within their organization or ministry, but in every case they know the pulse of the institution and have a feel for developments within the wider evangelical movement.

In all cases, the interviews were strictly confidential and the interviewees' names have been withheld, though transcripts were made of the interviews. Approximately half of the interviews were conducted in person and the other half by telephone. Interviews averaged from thirty to sixty minutes.

The interviews were open-ended discussions. The interviewees were asked to address how they perceived the general state of evangelicalism at the close of the twentieth century. Each were given four questions to discuss: Who are evangelicals? What is the state of evangelicalism? Where are evangelicals going? Who are the leaders of evangelicalism?

EIGHT DOMINANT THEMES

What follows are the discussions and illustrations of the eight dominant themes that emerged in these discussions. In some cases, not all of the findings are illustrated specifically, especially if telling quotes are used elsewhere in this book.

1. Uncertain identity

Evangelical leaders expressed a widespread uncertainty over what constitutes an evangelical. They had a weakened commitment to the movement and its institutions.

- "There seems to be three factions within evangelicalism today—those oriented around theology [represented by seminaries], those that are oriented around sociology [represented by the church-growth movement], and those oriented around renewal [represented by the charismatic and prayer movements]."—*Denomination executive*

- "I'm not overly excited about where my denomination is going, but I'm not a Jeremiah about it either. . . . Some folks like me will finally say we're really more at home in one of the old historic traditions, whether trying to find a middle way in the Episcopal church, or some who end up going to Rome, because they are so depressed over the state of Protestantism. I really feel those pulls profoundly."—*Pastor*

- "I don't think the evangelical community really understands what it means to be 'born again.' I don't know how many evangelicals you know who do. Maybe you identify with that community yourself. I don't. I identify more with the Catholic community." —*Christian college graduate and parachurch executive*

- "I've read *Evangelicals on the Canterbury Trail* and *Becoming Orthodox*. . . . It was not just cathartic for me. It told me that other people were having to deal with exactly what I was dealing with, so that was very affirming. . . . There are some people who just absolutely don't relate to why somebody would become Anglican or Catholic or Orthodox—but I think that a person who is more thinking-oriented is a person who seeks back toward early Christianity."—*Parachurch executive*

- "So I'm obviously a little bit sour on evangelicalism right now. And I know that there are massive problems anywhere else you go. There's no panacea. But where will I be granted more of the freedom to be the man that I believe God has called me to be in Christ Jesus? And I'm not sure it will be forever here."—*Pastor*

- "The state of the union to me is that over the years I have become increasingly dissatisfied with the superficiality of evangelicalism. It is too much of a closed circle; it is too predictable; it is too much based on celebrity speakers or authors."—*Parachurch executive*

- "There is little that I find appealing in the evangelical church. I find it fatiguing."—*Best-selling author*

Significance: Uncertainties about evangelicalism have been widespread, but until recently they have been limited mainly to scholars and defectors. That those who bear the institutional responsibility to shape the future of evangelicalism expressed this level of dissatisfaction candidly is a telling sign of the state of the evangelical identity. Evangelical leaders face a major challenge in reformulating the defining features of evangelicalism by which it is identified, united, and directed.

2. Institutional disenchantment

Evangelical leaders revealed a growing disenchantment with
evangelical institutions—including denominations, seminaries,
colleges, and Christian publishing. This took two forms. On the
one hand, they openly acknowledged a growing dissatisfaction
with evangelical institutions at large; on the other hand, they
were equally emphatic about the evangelical institutions' growing personal irrelevance to themselves.

- "Well, I don't read *Christianity Today* nearly as carefully
  as I used to, because I just find most of it to be not to
  the point. I have several times canceled, and then felt
  that I need to take it in the same way that I need to
  take *Newsweek*."—*Pastor*

- "[I'm] trying to find a place of grace in my own life to
  tolerate the church—to tolerate evangelicalism, as it
  were. And at the same time to live and hold dear the
  principles it's supposed to be representing. It's a hard
  thing."—*Foundation executive*

- "I have lived in the circle [the evangelical subculture]
  for so long that literally school, church, work, everything was evangelical. So I had to get in a church. . .
  where Jim Dobson's name wasn't brought up, where
  Chuck Swindoll's name wasn't brought up, where Christian radio wasn't brought up. I mean it was just like,
  here were normal unpretentious people who didn't know
  or care much about capital "E" evangelicalism. Because
  that was like work."—*Parachurch leader*

- "[The megachurch pastors] do not think it is popular to
  be a member of a denomination, or to be under the discipline of a denomination. . . . This is a crisis point for
  the evangelical community, whether it's going to continue to have denominations and put any importance

in them, or whether its going to abandon the idea."
—*Journalist*

- "There was so much about fundamentalist attitudes that to me wasn't Christian at all, so I became restless within the evangelical church."—*Parachurch leader*

- "I talked to a megachurch pastor about becoming president of a seminary, and he feels he's skilled at training people, and equipping them for the ministry, and all the things they do to equip their own, and more and more of these churches are going to produce their own seminaries—thank-you-very-much. . . . They want to train their own people. Not in theology, but in practical techniques."—*Magazine editor*

- "By and large our educational institutions are so thoroughly confused theologically that they are almost immobilized from giving any sense of direction at all."
—*College president*

- "I have a dim view of evangelical seminaries for this reason, that they are caught up in modernity regarding methods. . . . The evangelical seminaries have, like the liberal seminaries—the evangelical seminaries are a little worse, but only a little worse—they are becoming teaching factories, where in-depth research and study, life and contemplation, all of these things are regarded with suspicion. They are looking simply for results. They are oriented toward growth and the expansion of their program." —*Seminary professor*

- "We don't even have one bastion of intellectual leadership. We've got some good colleges, but even a Wheaton College—it may even get a higher percentage of its graduates into medical schools than Harvard or Yale—but Wheaton and Harvard are not debating at the same level." —*College president*

- "I think there is precious little thinking going on today. I think the reason is that the books that are hyped and the books that sell and the sermons that are preached and basically the entire evangelical ethos, is one of second-rate thinking and second-rate dreams." —*Pastor*

- "The problem is that most Christian publishing is brain-dead. . . . In the Christian world, there are very few books that you can pick up that are intellectually stimulating. The publishers are continually aiming lower and lower, and making it what we consider more popular. They just aren't really chewing on issues and thinking." —*Media expert*

- "My denomination speaks with some pride of our 'ministry to intellectuals.' And you listen to them and just say, 'Good grief!' They don't write well. They don't think well. And they don't seem to have read anything in the twentieth century that wasn't written by a fellow believer or someone who saw things very much the way they do. Or some schlock." —*Pastor*

Significance: This institutional disenchantment reveals the depth of the evangelical malaise that now amounts to a crisis of authority—evangelicals' loss of belief in their own institutions and distinctives. Evangelicalism appears to be running on past momentum. No religious community can sustain such disillusionment by its leadership for long, for it undercuts the necessary will to meet these challenges. The integrity and effectiveness of evangelicalism as a movement depend on a recovery of the harmony between identity, theology, institutions, and leadership.

3. Lament over leadership

Many of the leaders expressed deep concern over the lack of leadership within the church. Particularly missing is leadership that has a statesmen-like concern for the whole of the evangelical movement. Several explanatory factors were suggested—

the transition to a new generation of leaders, the impact of the sixties on these leaders, and their preoccupation with their own entrepreneurial enterprises.

- "I'm not sure evangelicalism is in any better shape than the country is, as far as leadership is concerned."—*Parachurch leader*

- Question: "Who are the most influential people today who are shaping the direction of evangelicalism?" Answer: "Oh, my word. . . My answer I think is nobody. And that's part of the problem. It's amazing the lack of leadership. It's a bunch of personalities who either are so hung up on their own kingdoms, on the one hand, or are so wrong-headed—so anti-intellectual that the very things we're sitting here and talking about are just outside their purview."—*Former NAE leader*

- "The guys you see listed on the masthead of *Leadership*, and the CT people, are probably pretty widely recognized as among the core of evangelical leaders. And there are some lovely people. I mean, I think they are probably all lovely Christian men and women, but I just don't see them as providing the kind of leadership that I need at all."—*Pastor*

- "As you move across the country—and I get to a lot of seminaries and colleges—we've got an amazing number of keen minds, but we don't have a personality with, say, 'Here you are, follow this person.' "—*Parachurch leader*

- "I've become much more aware of the shortage of leadership in a certain age category from the mid-forties to the mid-fifties, the period when people move into positions of leadership. [Most] of the gifted people are using those gifts to build their own kingdom and are rather oblivious of others."—*Member of a seminary presidential search committee*

- "The real leaders of evangelicalism are not the heads of the denominations, but the heads of these parachurch ministries."—*Foundation executive*

- "We need free agents—people not tied to existing organizations who can assert leadership during this time of transition. Don't rely on the institutions to provide leaders or make changes fast enough."—*Denomination executive*

- "The bigger question is, 'What do we want?' Do we want any leaders at all? Are we willing to have any? Are we running so gun-shy about those who have fallen that we're afraid to put up anybody to do anything, lest he fall also?"—*Journalist*

Significance: These comments are particularly telling because of their source. The lack of leadership was a lament by the evangelical leaders themselves. Modern American evangelicalism was shaped by the vision of numerous men and women in the 1940s. But today's leaders are frequently managers of the status quo rather than visionaries who could effect change for the movement as a whole. A few of the leaders even wonder aloud whether such leadership is either possible, desirable, or necessary in our modern context.

Evangelicalism faces a further series of questions that need to be addressed: Who will emerge as the new leaders? How should evangelical leaders work in concert? How will new leadership be encouraged under the fragmented conditions of American evangelicalism and the dislocated conditions of modern life?

4. Pessimism about the future

The evangelical leaders interviewed were openly ambivalent about the future of evangelicalism. On the one hand, they were pessimistic as to whether the movement had a future. But on the other hand, they were largely unconcerned about this prospect.

- "I'm not optimistic."—*Denomination executive*

- "My bottom-line gut feeling is that we're not going to turn evangelicalism around."—*Magazine editor*

- "Whether evangelicals can do anything really significant or not remains to be seen."—*NAE leader*

- "The evangelical movement runs the risk of being irrelevant to the future of our national history. What I see now within the evangelical community is an abandonment to materialism and Enlightenment thinking that is really at war with what I think of as being orthodox."
  —*Parachurch leader*

- "The problem is much deeper than evangelicals want to admit. We are now living in a secularist society. There is little hope of rejuvenating America with a resurgent evangelicalism."—*College president*

Significance: The pronounced absence of a sense of direction and hope is further evidence of the extent of evangelicalism's crisis of identity. A vital evangelicalism requires leaders who believe in its future, have a clear grasp of the direction in which they would like to see it go, and are committed to give their lives and fortunes to this task. If without vision the people perish, without hope there are no prospects for vision.

5. Growth up, impact down

Regarding the nature of the current situation, evangelical leaders were considerably confused. Some noted the stark contrasts between foreign opportunities and domestic problems. Others noted the disparities between the still-high statistical indicators of belief in America and the obviously declining social influence of the Christian faith.

- "I have to conclude that while evangelicalism appears to be growing in strength—our denominations are growing the fastest, and so on—our nation at the same time is on the slippery slope toward decadence, and as far as I'm concerned, that doesn't compute." —*NAE leader*

- "Evangelicals have a growth in statistics and finances, but a loss of substance. . . . They are not becoming liberal, but substanceless—an a-theological mirroring of the larger society." —*Southern Baptist leader*

- "We haven't done it all by ourselves, of course, but letting our country go down the drain is going to mean God's judgment and thus we'll be unable to continue as a force for world evangelism."—*Parachurch leader*

Significance: This confusion is significant because it takes place at a time of growing respectability for polling, demographic statistics, and pop futurism among evangelicals. Characteristic of bits-and-pieces thinkers, many evangelicals still see only the trees rather than the forest, the facts rather than the broader framework that is needed to make sense of the situation. Above all, evangelicals display a serious absence of an understanding of the broader challenges of modernity.

6. Awareness of cultural isolation

Evangelical leaders are concerned about evangelicals' isolation within their own subculture and the perceived irrelevance and hypocrisy to the broader culture. For some, the concern issued a feeling of open frustration at their fellow evangelicals combined with a sense of embarrassment over how intelligent outside observers perceive evangelicals.

- "The abuse evangelical leaders are taking from the unsaved, the unchurched community, is because they are really a farce. They're not suffering for righteous deeds and being accused and so forth for righteousness sake. They're suffering because of all the ridiculous and stupid and unrighteous things they've done to bring disgrace on the name of the body of Christ."—*Foundation executive*

- "The church is suffering from a kind of defensive parochialism right now, and consequently fails to be as creative as it ought to be."—*Parachurch executive*

- "I think the evangelical movement today is majoring in minors. We have elevated sectarian themes to essential themes. We have the gospel, but we have the gospel plus other ideas that are put on the same level as the gospel."—*Seminary professor*

- "The evangelical message has become more universal in terms of awareness, especially through missions and relief and service programs abroad, but we still have a tendency to be much more American and parochial than is wise. . . ."—*College president*

- "The Christian school movement, from top to bottom, from Christian colleges to Christian day schools and home schooling—while there are notable exceptions— I think far from giving a Christian worldview, it has given an aberrant, separatistic, ghetto mentality, which has kept us from impacting the universities, which impact everything."—*Pastor*

- "My great fear is that the students that we graduate, because they typically come from sort of middle-class families, will never have the opportunities to really shape the institutions of society that maybe the graduates of Harvard will have. . . . What's desperately needed is to somehow get the elite people in this country to think reformation."—*College president*

- "I don't think anybody believes that Campus Crusade or Inter-Varsity college students are necessarily going to have a vision of how to restore evangelicalism in America, or even restore America. They're sort of helping kids keep their faith in college—and that's the sort of narrow vision most people feel."—*College president*

- "It seems like evangelicals are completely out of touch with society. They are so entangled in their own doctrinal exercises, and arrogant and proud demonstrations of their own holiness and their own particular theological stance, that they are basically a meaningless discussion as it pertains to society in general."—*Foundation executive*

- "We have to break away from the old fortress mentality, the monastery approach, get our salt out of the shaker—the church—and into our society."—*Parachurch executive*

Significance: This frustration and embarrassment reveal the leaders' awareness of the broad changes in the wider culture, the wider audience before which evangelicals are now speaking, and the increasing irrelevance of the evangelical institutions and methodologies created in the forties and fifties. It is notable that in these private conversations the leaders had little resentment toward "cultural elites," "liberal media," or "secular humanists," even though this is frequently found in their direct-mail communications. Evangelical leaders were privately more willing to take responsibility for their irrelevance in culture. This acceptance may suggest a new stage in the evangelical public consciousness and a new starting point for the search for alternative responses.

7. Two main responses

Evangelical leaders' response to evangelical isolation and ineffectiveness in culture tended to take two directions: the first was political, by drawing on the traditional evangelical reliance on grassroots mobilization; and the second was structural, by using the insights and techniques of management and marketing in order to make the church more relevant to modern people. The leaders interviewed were almost equally divided between those supporting and those criticizing these two approaches. They generally agreed that the structural approach, as seen in the megachurch movement, has the greatest momentum within evangelicalism.

- "Sometimes Christians have been spiritual and intellectual wimps when it comes down to pressing for the values that we know are for the good of the nation. . . . We don't know our own strength. If two-thirds of evangelicals voted for the losing candidate the results of the presidential elections of 1948, 1960, 1968, and 1976 could have been overturned."—*NAE leader*

- "We have not thought through what our common evangelical view is of the role of the gospel and culture. . . . Are we trying to return to the golden age of a 'Christian America'? We haven't nailed that coffin shut—which I think it ought to be. Are we seeking to go back to the 1940s and what some sociologists and historians have called the hegemony of white, Anglo-Saxon Protestant males?"—*College president*

- "I had been saddened years ago belonging to a denomination that became a house-organ for the Democratic party, and I pray that the Lord will deliver my present denomination from becoming a house-organ of the Republican party, because it's the same thing. And I see that kind of thinking permeating the church, a belief in political solutions."—*Pastor*

LEFT   /   RIGHT
POLITICAL SOLUTIONS   /   ECONOMIC
                               SOLUTIONS

- "I see what I call restorationism in the evangelical camp, the return to past positions. . . . It's always trying to retrieve the past rather than speak to burning issues in the present. But there is something more sinister in it, and I think it is this, that it's an attempt to gain an additional certainty for faith beyond the certainty that faith itself provides. They want to be shored up by the past."—*Seminary professor*

- "The structural reformation is being led in the large churches, and is being more or less ignored by seminaries. . . . Seminaries perceive themselves to be in a very confused state, and in disarray, and in bad shape. Several of them are worried about financial survival, and really questioning their niche and role."—*Megachurch consultant*

- "Evangelicalism is focused on how can man's needs be met and how God can make you a happy camper. American evangelicalism is based on a self-serving theology."—*Parachurch board member*

- "What is happening is that people who are operating churches, which are more complex than simply teaching institutions or ritual places, are now going by the thousands to hear people who are operating big churches. . . . The reason they are going is because what they are interested in knowing is how to do church, rather than answering theological or doctrinal questions." —*Megachurch consultant*

- "Are we really supposed to have $100,000 pumped into a sports ministry? Are we really supposed to be doing all these things that put our walls up high? Aren't we supposed to be worshiping and then going out into the world? My children keep asking, 'What does this have to do with the incarnation of Jesus Christ?' I think that this megachurch trend is probably all going to backfire.

I think that I may well be helping to build a thing here that will be empty twenty-five or thirty years from now."—Large-church pastor

- "The church is 90 percent structurally still operating in the old paradigm. The new paradigm responds to the question: 'What if the church were defined by its results, not by its events or processes?' "—*Megachurch consultant*

- "The market-driven movement within the evangelical church has a dynamic of its own. The evangelical church is characterized by the self-fulfillment ethic and the reign of the therapeutic to a larger degree than the secular culture. And it's lost a sense of guilt about this."—*Southern Baptist seminary president*

Significance: The leaders disagreed about which approach is best. The two approaches have important differences between them— the political strategy looks more to the past, to a lost golden age, while the structural approach looks more to the future, as it is ever changing to meet the new market opportunities and felt needs. But what is strikingly absent in both alternatives is any confidence in traditional theology. The apparent losers in the present discussions are the institutions of traditional theological education.

8. Shifting prerequisites for leadership

The leaders frequently mentioned the apparent shift in the qualifications considered necessary for leadership within evangelical organizations—from truth-centered to market-responsive criteria. This change adds to the devaluation of theological thinking and traditional seminary education within evangelicalism.

- "The tendency today in the evangelical world is to do whatever it takes to see growth. And I think that they are tickling themselves with fantasies of grandeur

TRUTH -CENTERED
MARKET- RESPONSIVE

through a compromise of truth."—*Parachurch board member*

- "I think we're losing the mind of the culture, where we're emphasizing—as in the megachurch movement—shaping of attitudes, emotions, personal growth, but not theology. And unless we define our faith over against the world in such a way that the world will take notice, we will lose the mind of the culture. We're changing hearts, but not the minds of the people."—*Seminary professor*

- "A program that tells the truth doesn't make it on the radio. It's a program that gives you self-help—how to understand yourself better and how to understand your kids better. . . . It's a 'I'm OK, you're OK' and 'let's make us better people.' It's not 'if we lose ourselves in Christ then he will set us free.'"—*Evangelical author*

- "The church-growth movement is living on borrowed theological capital, and it is unlikely to be able to sustain its theological perspective over the subsequent generation."—*Denomination executive*

- "I really feel that the evangelical church must take seriously the biblical illiteracy of our time, the lack of knowledge, of thoughtful reflection about God. . . . This is partly due to education, and also partly due to the way churches have shifted to try to compete more with Hollywood entertainment, than really doing solid teaching."—*Journalist*

- "The lack of theological work on the part of evangelicals is in my judgment nothing short of scandalous. . . . Here are the facts: The theology committee of the National Association of Evangelicals has met once in the past six years. I mean, case closed. We say we are committed to the infallibility and the authority of Scripture. What does that really mean?"—*Former NAE leader*

- "I've told several seminary presidents that I think most of the graduates from seminary that I know do not have a well-integrated biblical world and life view."—*College president*

Significance: The widespread devaluing of truth, theology, and theological education illustrates the move away from traditional confessional evangelicalism and from those institutions concerned with its preservation. While market-driven evangelicalism thrives in the short-term, the factors contributing to its success may simultaneously corrupt its spiritual vitality. And so evangelicalism may be responsible for digging its own grave.

THE THREE CRISES OF EVANGELICALISM

These findings can be summarized by three crises: first, a crisis of authority, which is a loss of belief in evangelical institutions and distinctives; second, a crisis of impact, which is an awareness of an isolation from and impotence within American society; and third, a crisis of response, which is a widespread disagreement over how to proceed.

A crisis of authority. Once again consider the statement by a baby-boomer leader who graduated from a Christian college and Wheaton College Graduate School, as well as being president of multiple parachurch organizations: "I don't think the evangelical community really understands what it means to be 'born again.' I don't know how many evangelicals you know who do. Maybe you identify with that community yourself. I don't. I identify more with the Catholic community."

Two aspects of his comment are telling. First, he criticized evangelicals for not appreciating or understanding what it means to be "born again." Historically this has been the defining experience of evangelicals. And so he suggested that evangelicals' ignorance of this crucial concept is the most explicit example of evangelicalism's corruption. Second, though I had been told by others that this leader was an evangelical and from his past insti-

tutional associations I expected this to be true, instead he said
that he identified with the Catholic tradition. In fact, he even
expressed surprise that I still identify with the evangelical community. He, as others I interviewed, assumed that thinking Christians would be abandoning the movement.

A *crisis of impact*. Look again at the statement of a Christian
college president who openly acknowledged the limitations of
Christian education: "We don't even have one bastion of intellectual leadership. We've got some good colleges, but even a
Wheaton College—it may even get a higher percentage of its
graduates into medical schools than Harvard or Yale—but
Wheaton and Harvard are not debating at the same level."

His comment demonstrates a unique breath of perspective
among evangelical leaders. He evaluated evangelical institutions
from outside of evangelicalism. He has recognized that the success of evangelical institutions can be measured in many ways.
Evangelical institutions are usually compared with other evangelical institutions, which distorts their real cultural impact. Students may receive a fine education from evangelical colleges.
But in contrast to the secular learning institutions that shape
the opinion leaders and institutional gatekeepers of public life,
this leader admitted that even the best Christian colleges play in
a different league.

A *crisis of response*. No one leader summarized neatly the
varying types of responses within evangelicalism. The polariza-
tions varied between political activism versus evangelism, theology versus technique. One seminary professor suggested that
many of the approaches evangelicals follow are an "attempt to
gain an additional certainty for faith beyond the certainty that
faith itself provides." This is true of many of the approaches,
whether politically oriented or managerially oriented.

A denominational president did not hesitate when asked to
describe the dominant factions within evangelicalism: "There
seem to be three factions within evangelicalism today—those
oriented around theology, those oriented around sociology, and
those oriented around renewal."

By theology, he referred not only to traditional seminaries, but to all those who advocate the importance of theology. He went on to discuss how theology has been increasingly marginalized in evangelicalism. By sociology, he made a loose reference to the megachurch movement and its use of market analysis and statistics. He noted the growing appeal of the movement within his denomination and the growth of special training seminars for pastors. He also mentioned the broader charismatic movement with his term "renewal." The lack of a wider mention of the charismatic movement in the interviews is probably due to the size and composition of the sample. But the charismatic movement itself is divided between theology and technique.

Evangelicals' concern for evangelism and experience makes them naturally oriented toward results. And so it is not surprising that advocates of techniques that promise growth and converts are attracting a growing following. This denominational president understood the trends clearly. He is among a growing number of leaders who are trying to make sense of the significance of these pushes and pulls within the movement.

These findings give evidence of a growing crisis within evangelicalism. Evangelicalism is in transition. With an absence of unifying leadership and clear identity, evangelicals are jockeying for positions of authority. It is to these turf wars that we now turn.

Handwritten annotations:

EVANGELISM   THEOLOGY
ACTIVISM   TECHNIQUE

↑ ↓ IMPORTANCE OF THEOLOGY
, " " MARKET ANALYSIS
. , " " SPIRITUAL GROWTH

POLITICALLY ORIENTED
PSYCHOLOGICALLY "
MANAGERIALLY "

Questions for Reflection and Discussion

1. From your own knowledge and experience, answer the questions posed to these evangelical leaders: Who are evangelicals? What is the state of evangelicalism? Where are evangelicals going? Who are the leaders of evangelicalism?

2. After listening to these leaders, what is your assessment of the future of evangelicalism?

3. What constructive steps forward would you suggest?

BLUE PLAYING FOR ETERNAL STAKES
RED PLAYING FOR MATERIAL/TEMPORAL STAKES
YELLOW PLAYING FOR SPIRITUAL/TEMPORAL STAKES

4

PLAYING FOR DIFFERENT STAKES

> "Players can play to increase or to conserve their capital, their number of tokens, in conformity with the tacit rules of the game and its stakes; but they can also get in to transform, partially or completely, the rules of the game."
>
> —Pierre Bourdieu

"IT WAS WARFARE"

LEADERS AT EVANGELICAL SEMINARIES became curious when they heard that a high-level group of megachurch leaders planned to meet in Colorado Springs in April of 1991. Originally, the megachurch leaders had designed the meeting to offer a context for an informal exchange of ideas among pastors of megachurches. But the plans were changed because of the seminary leaders' interest.

It was hardly surprising that the leaders of the seminaries—the traditional source of pastoral training and credentials—were curious. For megachurch conferences, sponsored by "teaching-model" churches, are becoming major competitors in pastoral training.

A megachurch consultant described a teaching-model church as "a large church that actively and intentionally tries to assist the growth and ministry of other churches, and/or a church to which pastors and other church leaders frequently come to learn more about improving the effectiveness of their own ministries."[1] In the past, evangelical teaching-model churches would have been known more typically for making biblical exposition a priority—such as Tenth Presbyterian Church in Philadelphia under Donald Grey Barnhouse or All Soul's Church in London under the ministry of John Stott.

These three- to five-day conferences for pastors and members of the church leadership have proliferated in recent years. Approximately three thousand pastors attended the 1992 training programs of Willow Creek Community Church, in South Barrington, Illinois, with several overseas conferences scheduled. Over eleven thousand church leaders have attended the training provided by Skyline Wesleyan Church of San Diego and over twelve thousand pastors have attended the Saddleback Church Growth Conferences of Saddleback Valley Community Church in Mission Viejo, California.

But the April 1991 meeting differed from the norm. Instead of being an exchange of ideas for teaching the megachurch model, it became an "intervention experience" for seminary leaders as they began to realize the extent of the megachurch challenge. One participant summarized the seminary leaders' reaction to the meeting: "Good grief! There's a different way to learn this, and we're not doing it!" Joe Aldridge, president of Multnomah School of the Bible, is said to have lamented publicly, "A [seminary] faculty is harder to move than a cemetery." This comment describes the dilemma of having a fixed curriculum, fixed teaching method, fixed length of course work, and fixed piece of real estate.

At the conclusion of the meeting, the participants scheduled a second meeting for November of 1991. Seminaries were encouraged to invite the chairman of their board of trustees, the president, and an influential graduate of whom the seminary was proud. After the meeting, descriptions of the time together varied from a megachurch advocate's comment that it was "a time of some notable tension" to a Christian and Missionary Alliance denominational executive stating flatly, "It was warfare." The meeting concluded with six seminaries jointly commissioning a private study of large churches' assessment of seminaries. They were trying to determine the seriousness of a potential institutional bypass. The seminaries were on the defensive. This defensiveness was the result of such statements as the following made by one of the organizers of the meeting:

> I believe there is a bifurcation which is taking place right now in the teaching of religion, between the science of religion and the practice of religion, with the science of religion being taught in an academic setting. The practice of religion is evolving so quickly that it's difficult for a seminary to teach that—because it's a moving target. . . . And given the fact that we live in times of uncertainty, unpredictability, turbulence, and radical change, the failure to be pretty adaptive is terminal.
>
> The teaching churches are highly adaptive, and the questions most people are asking, I think I can say with great confidence now, are questions that deal with how to convert belief into action, or how to convert theology into behavior, rather than questions that deal with the purity of theology.[2]

Advocates of the megachurch movement frequently describe the shift between teaching theology and teaching the practice of religion in hyperbolic terms. Consider the following statements: "The forms and structures, the roles and relationships of the churches we have inherited were formed by paradigms that no longer work for us," states mainline church consultant, Loren Mead. "The North American church is in an upheaval not seen in three hundred years, because it is restless with old forms," says megachurch consultant David Schmidt. "You can't have innovative break-throughs without a break with tradition. . . the way we have always done it," adds megachurch pastor, Rick Warren. Or consider a more blunt statement about the traditional church by Leadership Network—an informal megachurch think tank—in a brochure for a 1993 conference: "When the horse is dead, dismount."

Paradigm shifts. . . upheaval. . . breaking with tradition. . . dismounting. These are strong challenges to the evangelical establishment. A gauntlet has been thrown down by the megachurch movement. What significance does this conflict between megachurches and seminaries hold? What is at stake? How does it illustrate the other types of turf battles and shifting alliances taking place within evangelicalism?

THREE TYPES OF TURF BATTLES

Within any social community, struggles to define a group's identity and direction are inevitable. Some of the struggles are overt and involve public clashes between strong individuals or institutions; others are covert, involving behind-the-scenes coalitions or informal relationships that shape institutional priorities or the allocation of resources. Sometimes these battles are symbolized by a single event—an explosive test of wills—but more normally they are the conclusion of small, incremental decisions made over a long period of time. When a group self-consciously tries to maintain or change a social community it is often the most successful when it follows a slow course of change, through the unconscious acceptance of the community. For whoever influences the taken-for-granted assumptions of a community controls its future.

Evangelicalism is just such a community. Because there is no evangelical magisterium, no official ruling body, broad shifts in the recognized leadership, the institutional priorities, and the communal identity can go unnoticed. Quite often it is difficult to see a pattern emerge from the mosaic of disparate theological traditions, parachurch ministries, and ethnic communities.

But sociologists observe that three distinct types of turf battles frequently take place in any social community. Each of these turf battles, which we will explore below, are simultaneously apparent within evangelicalism. These turf battles point to the extent of turmoil taking place within the movement.

Perhaps the easiest way to illustrate these types of turf battles is to describe a game of cards—Rook, for example, since it was the only card game allowed on the mission field historically. Rook is played with four colored suits—red, green, yellow, and black—and one wild Rook card. Players bid on the strength of their hand for the right to declare the color of trump and to lead the playing of the hand. The strength of a player's hand can shift instantly if another person calls a suit trump in which the player has only a few cards.

The options available to players in a card game, such as Rook, parallel the options facing those who provide leadership to a particular social group. One option is simply to play out the cards in one's hand. Little is risked by this strategy, but when carefully played it can thwart others who expose themselves to greater risks. A second option is to bid for the right to declare trump, to shift the value of the cards toward those one already possesses. This, of course, means taking risks—bidding the highest for the right to take leadership in the game. A third option, and one that is itself a strategy in such games as poker, is simply to fold or change the game—either the rules of the game or the game itself.

The turf battles within evangelicalism involve players that are opting for each of these three strategies. We will examine each strategy more closely, looking at examples of their dominant expression within evangelicalism.

PLAYING A WINNING HAND

The first approach maintains the status quo. The evangelical leaders who opt for this strategy are similar to the card players who accept the rules of the game without question. They play the hand dealt to them without bidding for trump, seeking to improve their position within the game on this basis alone. These leaders assume the past resources of evangelicalism and seek to position evangelicals within the broader cultural struggle on the basis of these long-established and institutionalized strengths.

This strategy can be seen best in those who appeal to grassroots political mobilization as the means to further the evangelical cause.

We could point to many potential illustrations of political activism within evangelicalism. Since the mid-1970s, politics has been the dominant means through which evangelicals have sought to regain cultural dominance. Such organizations as the Moral Majority, Concerned Women for America, Christian Coalition, Family Research Council, Traditional Values Coalition, or many other national and regional organizations are evangelicals' instrument through which family values and a biblical worldview are advocated in the public square.

These organizations frequently rely on the strength of evangelical populism, particularly the history of political mobilization and moral agitation. An example of this approach, and one of the more constructive recent efforts, is the Christian Citizenship Campaign sponsored during the 1992 election by the National Association of Evangelicals.

The NAE is a voluntary fellowship of evangelical denominations, churches, schools, organizations, and individuals. It is both a voice and a forum for American evangelicals. Today, more than fifty years after its founding, the NAE speaks for about 15 million evangelicals. It is a cooperative fellowship of almost forty-five thousand local churches from seventy-five denominations, over two hundred evangelical associations, organizations, and educational institutions, plus several thousand individual clergy and laity.

In the spring of 1992, at its fiftieth-anniversary convention, the NAE launched its first nationwide Christian Citizenship Campaign. They gave this initiative high visibility and importance. Robert P. Dugan, Jr., Director of NAE's Office of Public Affairs in Washington, D.C., said in the campaign's press release, "Nothing could be more appropriate than to take such a stride 'Forward in Faith' [the convention theme] at this moment. As we begin NAE's second half-century, our nation is caught in a profound culture war. Evangelical Christians possess the weapons to win that war."

Tim Crater, National Citizenship Chairman, stated that the purpose of the "non-partisan" campaign was to encourage churches to pray more specifically and knowledgeably for their political leaders, while registering a million voters. He said in the press release, "Never has the salt and light of evangelical influence been more needed in public life than now. The issues which affect the church and religious liberty are serious ones, as we increasingly confront the militant secularism of our culture. This is no time for Christian citizens to be apathetic or disengaged."

Although this campaign did not make a significant difference in national politics, it received broad support among key evangelical groups. The Southern Baptist Convention's Christian Life Commission strongly endorsed it and produced their own version of the training manual. And Robert Dugan was invited to be a guest on James Dobson's Focus on the Family radio show twice to discuss the campaign, thus securing maximum legitimacy within evangelical circles.

We will now examine this campaign by exploring three questions: What is being said? Who is saying it? What does it mean?

What is being said?

The campaign rhetoric appeals to four of the dominant evangelical dispositions examined in chapter two: roots, revival, resentment, and reassertion. Thus the campaign was positioned squarely within the American evangelical identity.

Appeal to roots. Equating "heavenly citizenship" with "earthly citizenship"—specifically American citizenship—is alluded to repeatedly in the campaign material. The manual quotes evangelical abolitionist Charles Finney, "God cannot sustain this free and blessed country which we love and pray for, unless the Church will take the right ground. Politics are a part of a religion in such a country as this, and Christians must do their duty to the country as a part of their duty to God. God will bless or curse

HEAVENLY CITIZENSHIP
EARTHLY CITIZENSHIP

this nation, according to the course they take."[3] In a sample sermon supplied in the campaign manual entitled "A Call for Christian Citizenship," we read,

> Would God be opposed to our using these hard-won privileges [democratic vote], which He Himself supplied, to defend the very lifestyle and Christian mission He commands us to fulfill? Hardly. It is far more likely that He will hold us accountable for our stewardship of these privileges. We should use the powers of our earthly citizenship in defense of both our heavenly callings [the evangelical way of life and the freedom to evangelize]."[4]

The vote is a tool and a responsibility within a democracy to be used in the service of furthering God's kingdom. But the notion of "Christian citizenship" can be easily confused if the priority of the kingdom of God is not clearly understood. And the potential for confusion is heightened if one assumes that America has a special status in God's redemptive plan, as is frequently the case among those who follow this strategy.

Appeal to revival. The manual reads, "The oft-cited promise of God to heal the land of His people (2 Chronicles 7:14) is based on the willingness of Christians to 'humble themselves *and pray.*' The need for another 'Great Awakening' in America is self-evident; fervent, faithful prayer for it is the prerequisite."[5] Elsewhere Dugan writes: "Ronald Reagan was fond of saying, 'The greatest revolution in history began with the words, 'We the people.' I believe the *greatest revival of a nation in history* must begin with the words, 'We the evangelicals.' "[6]

Appeal to resentment. A feeling of resentment over evangelicals' loss of cultural dominance lies behind the warlike tone of the material. The opening paragraph of the bulletin sent to NAE's National Legislative Alert Network read,

> Look around you. The smoke and noise of battle may not be evident, but there's a war going on—a culture war. In the United States, evangelical churches are confronting a mili-

tant secularism in 'a new civil war.' America's Founders would
be astounded to see today's widespread rejection of the traditional Jewish and Christian values upon which they built
this nation.[7]

The Christian Citizenship Campaign's aim was "to enlist an
all-volunteer army to win that war." The cultural conflict was
called a "menacing reality," and opponents "secular zealots."
Crater said in an interview, "The secular animosity toward things
of faith is intensifying, and now is the hour for the church to
stand up and say, 'Enough!' The state needs to get out of the
sanctuary—leave it alone—and more than that, we need to have
the salt and light of our values felt at the polls at election day."[8]

Appeal to reassertion. The entire campaign was premised on
the need to galvanize evangelical voters. Crater wrote, "One
reason for the encroachment of anti-Christian secularism is the
woeful lack of substantial Christian participation in American
public life." Against a background of declining involvement in
politics by American citizens, down to 50 percent participation,
Crater said that 26 percent of the vote has the clout of 51 percent. He explained, "It's just a matter of numbers. If only 50 percent vote, then half plus one rules. They pick the president and
so on."[9]

Elsewhere another member of the NAE called evangelicals
to engage in politics: "The coming civil war is at hand. The sol-
diers of decadence and ruin are marching, grimly determined to
reshape the nation in their own image. They can be stopped—
but not without a fight. Who will respond to God's trumpet blast
to battle? This is the evangelical hour. The time to choose has
come."[10]

Through this campaign, these evangelical leaders sought to
strengthen the power and perspective of an evangelical worldview within the larger society. They reasserted traditional evangelical strengths while assuming the validity of the given
evangelical identity. The secularization of the culture could be
reversed, they believed, through grassroots mobilization.

Consider this question: Was this campaign primarily spiritual or political? Its stated intention was clearly both. But note the unintended priority given to the political. In the press release the goal of prayer was summarized in nine words, while the entire political agenda took up the rest of the approximately five-hundred-word release. In the material sent to the National Legislative Alert Network, only one-sixth of the space was given to discussing the goal of increased prayer or other spiritual concerns. In the *Christian Citizenship Campaign: A Manual for ACTION*, only 15 percent of the forty-page manual was devoted to the goal of increased prayer.

When examined more closely, the material on prayer in both the manual and in a book that gave the foundation for the campaign did not serve a spiritual purpose, but was viewed as a means of voter education. "Who can imagine what God might do in response to the knowledgeable intercession of millions of evangelicals for their elected officials? I mean *intelligent* intercession."[11] But three paragraphs later, the reader discovers the real reason behind "intelligent intercession"—and it has little to do with prayer or our need for God's direct intervention.

> Intelligent prayer has a byproduct that leads directly to our second duty. As you pray, you may become aware that you are well served by one officeholder, but that another has a dependably disappointing voting record. The Lord seems to be answering some of your prayers, but not others. Since 'faith without deeds is dead,' after some months or years of praying, you might surprise yourself by joining a political campaign— maybe to keep one legislator or to dump the other.[12]

The campaign illustrates a renewal of grassroots mobilization—with voter registration advocated during worship services and pastoral admonitions from the pulpit. The unintended danger is that prayer is put on a par with responsibilities of citizenship. "For the same reasons we are told to pray, we should also exercise our rights as citizens," the manual stated.

One woman wrote to the NAE about what the campaign meant to her Christian and Missionary Alliance congregation. Her letter was circulated widely as a positive example of the value of the campaign. She wrote, "Because of your efforts, our congregation seems to have new hope that all is not lost. There is hope for our land IF we band together as Christians and do what we can. That is what we are trying to do in our small corner of America and I just pray that others are doing the same thing." The message of this campaign is that evangelical confidence is based on political power.

Who is saying it?

The campaign is especially important because it was carried out under the auspices of the NAE. The NAE's institutional strength is located in evangelical denominations, particularly Pentecostal denominations, rather than in parachurch organizations. Consequently the campaign was church-based. It was one program of a voluntary association whose mission is to serve its constituents.

But it is equally instructive to note that the two identifiable leaders of this campaign are both former Baptist pastors. Tim Crater gave up his church in Atlanta to campaign for U.S. Representative Pat Swindoll. Robert Dugan gave up his church in suburban Denver in 1976 to run unsuccessfully for the U.S. House of Representatives.

With the closing of the Moral Majority and the weakening of the religious right, this was an opportune moment for the NAE to assert its leadership, particularly on the occasion of its fiftieth anniversary. Though the NAE's headquarters are located in Wheaton, Illinois, the Office of Public Affairs in Washington is the more public face of the organization.

What does it mean?

This campaign appealed to the traditional strength of American evangelicals—grassroots mobilization and political populism. It created the expectation that the culture war could be won by the political ballot. In doing so, it failed to take into account the radical nature of the cultural shift in American society. Like others who advocate political strategies in isolation from cultural strategies, the campaign failed to acknowledge that nineteenth-century populist political reform strategies will not expand evangelical influence in national life at the end of the twentieth century.

What was the real purpose of the campaign? Was it to increase voter registration and participation or was the campaign basically symbolic? From the outset, the campaign appeared to have little chance of success. For all the press coverage, there were no practical means of implementing its goals or measuring its results. No follow-up was planned—in spite of statements that church-based Citizenship Committees needed to be an ongoing feature of evangelical churches—and there was no ongoing strategy for after the 1992 election year. The Christian Citizenship Campaign illustrates how good intentions alone are not enough to ensure cultural impact.

The campaign was marked by two characteristics—a nostalgia for the past and a preoccupation with the symbolic. The campaign was premised on the desire to use political legislation and leadership to win back American culture to values and perspectives consistent with its Judeo-Christian heritage. And by adopting strategies frequently used by Jessie Jackson and other black leaders, they hoped that evangelicals would emerge as a voting bloc with serious national clout.

After Bill Clinton was elected few were confident of the campaign's success. But even if a conservative president had been elected, even if evangelicals' voting patterns were proven decisive in selecting national political leaders, culture would not have been significantly altered. For politics, including legislation, does not change cultural direction. To return to our illustration of the card game, evangelicals' preoccupation with politics is like playing a hand of high cards in a suit other than trump. It was decisive in the past; it leads to failure in the present.

BLUE

And the unintended consequences of a politicized faith are not so benign. Frequently the political rationalism of modern evangelicals, with exit polls and majoritarian rhetoric, seems to replace spiritual confidence. The "spirit of political activism" is a powerful secularizing agent. By exaggerating the importance of politics in society—"how small, of all that human hearts endure, that part which laws or kings can cause or cure"—political action may eventually eclipse everything except temporal ends. Should that be the result, ideology will have replaced spirituality.

Many evangelical leaders advocate a narrowly political strategy and seek to make evangelicalism a more effective political weapon in the culture wars. At best, the resort to politics is only a strategy of defense. It may slow the cultural drift, but it will not redirect the culture.

Nonetheless, evangelicals continue to do what worked in the past. But our cultural context has changed, and those who rely on politics alone to change the culture do not take this factor into account. Relying on politics alone has the unintended danger of reducing us to an ideological political faction whose priorities are focused on our secondary citizenship and whose confidence is based on legislative gains.

CHOOSING A DIFFERENT TRUMP

The second approach directly challenges the status quo. Rather than assuming past resources to position itself in society, it bids to change the accepted cultural capital—in our game of cards, the trump suit. In doing so these evangelical leaders seek to discredit their opponents' resources while they promote their own. This high-risk strategy automatically calls into question the accumulated strengths and institutionalized resources of evangelical traditionalists. Moreover, it has the rhetorical advantage of appealing to such modern notions as change, relevance, and progress.

This strategy differs tactically from the first. Rather than directly confronting their opponents on the opponents' terms, they instead seek to define the opponents' long-established strengths as irrelevant. This is, in short, a flanking maneuver or institutional bypass. It frequently is the shortest route to establishing a position of influence within a social group, because one can build on already existing strengths. The slow process of forming a portfolio of educational or financial resources is not necessary when they are simply declared as irrelevant to social advancement, being replaced in importance by those resources already possessed. Trump, we could say, has been redefined.

This type of venture is extremely subversive to the power relations within a social community. It can instantly define vast accumulations of individual and institutional capital as irrelevant. Moreover, as in all flanking movements, once momentum has been achieved in the process of revaluing the preferred resources, the opponent, who has positioned the forces for a frontal assault, becomes progressively limited in the ability to respond because of a lack of either institutional flexibility or diversity of resources.

This second strategy can be best illustrated by the megachurch movement. This is a growing phenomenon within evangelicalism, marked by large, mall-sized superchurches that aggressively apply business techniques in response to burgeoning religious consumerism. Today approximately forty-three of these Protestant congregations in the United States claim five thousand or more Sunday worshipers.

With the declining significance of denominations both in mainline Protestantism and evangelicalism, these "Christian emporiums" rival in size and influence all of the institutional structures of evangelical Protestantism. Moreover, megachurch leaders frequently question the legitimacy of more traditional churches and seminaries by changing the value of the preferred resources—the trump suit—within pastoral leadership.

Thus the megachurch movement is more than just a passing fad or a congealing of sunbelt religious fervor. The future institutional landscape of American Protestantism and the collective identity of evangelicalism are at stake in its bid for ascendancy.

What is being said?

The megachurch movement applies the three dominant modern revolutions—management, therapeutic, and communications—to the process of "doing church." Church is analyzed as a service business by megachurch advocates. Marketing consultant George Barna, for example, says that church is "the transaction in service of felt needs."[13] The four "Ps" of marketing follow naturally: product, price, place, and promotion. For example, Barna describes the church's task solely in marketing categories—the product is relationships (with Jesus and others); price is commitment; place is with believers, promotion is word-of-mouth.[14]

Traditional churches are severely criticized for their lack of market sensitivity and savvy. They are variously described as backward, boring, superficial, ritualistic, and embarrassing.[15] In short, they are said to have an inward product-orientation rather than an outward market-orientation.

In contrast, the new entrepreneurial churches, Leith Anderson writes, "are market-sensitive and attempt to take current trends and needs into consideration, using such up-to-date methodology as telemarketing, advertising, and high-tech communications. These churches seek to be highly relational. They plan to be big and offer full services from the start. Part of the attraction is the lack of tradition. There is no one to say, 'We've never done it that way before.' No creeds, no liturgy, no building, no history. Everything is new and fresh."[16]

Kenneth Woodward of *Newsweek* summarizes the church-growth phenomenon as the 1990s' response to "an age of mix'em, match'em salad-bar spirituality where brand loyalty is a doctrine of the past and the customer is king."[17] A minister's accountability is not finally based on doctrinal faithfulness, but on what one Baptist pastor described as "nickels and noses."

The megachurch movement has a wide diversity of approaches within it. But the movement as a whole can be summarized by the following three statements: The traditional church has been insular and ineffective; the new church must

DOCTRINAL FAITHFULNESS / NICKLES / NUMBERS / NOISE

INWARD   OUTWARD
PRODUCT   MARKET

break with traditional service patterns; and the new church must address felt-needs with a relevant message.

The old-paradigm church has been insular and ineffective. From the perspective of history, this assertion is sweepingly false—the nineteenth-century missionary movement is evidence enough to show its fallacy. But as American evangelicals have become aware of our insulation within the evangelical subculture, such statements create a sense of spiritual guilt. Our isolation, megachurch pastors suggest, belies our commitment to evangelism.

Thus by raising the guilt of isolation and the shame of ineffectiveness, megachurch advocates secure the attention of evangelical pastors, who already feel marginalized and defeated. This guilt is then ameliorated by the dual promise of effective evangelism and increased membership. For a struggling small church pastor, this can be an intoxicating combination. Bill Hybels says he built Willow Creek Community Church as a "last gasp effort." One senses that same desperate feeling in the pastors who crowd the growing number of "teaching church" seminars offered across the country.

The new-paradigm church must break with traditional service patterns. The church's problem is identified as primarily structural. An executive of Leadership Network repeats his conviction that the most profound change taking place today in the life of the church is a "reformation of structure." This organizational and institutional paradigm shift is being led by the new large "full-service," "designer," "seven-day-a-week," "entrepreneurial" superchurches. Church-growth consultant Bill Hendricks writes,

> All of this leads to a hypothesis, that large churches represent the future of the American church. The small church will always be around, just as local markets and convenience stores still dot the American landscape. But in terms of market penetration, innovation, and leadership, to say nothing of financial muscle, large churches will increasingly dominate.[18]

The megachurches are presented as the leading edge of the new ecclesiastical world order. *Compass*, a Leadership Network bulletin, poses this rhetorical question in a recent issue, "Are you living in the new world?" An executive of the organization notes sadly, "The church is 90 percent structurally still in the old paradigm."[19]

Acceptance of change is a prerequisite to be a part of the movement. "Given the fact that we live in times of uncertainty, unpredictability, turbulence, and radical change," says a megachurch leader, "the failure to be pretty adaptive is terminal."[20] Evangelicals are "dying for change," Anderson writes. Thus, "all 'man-made' traditions or biases were thrown out the window," writes James Mellado in a Harvard Business School Case Study of Willow Creek Community Church.[21] "We wanted to 'do church' in a different way," says Hybels.[22]

The new-paradigm church must address felt-needs with a relevant message. In answering the question of why the church is irrelevant and losing influence in society, Barna is straightforward: "Essentially, people have come to realize that many, if not most, of the Protestant churches in this country are not responding to people's felt needs. They are mired in tradition and not changing with the times, not on the cutting edge."[23]

Barna, the John Naisbitt of the megachurch movement, is the president of Barna Research Group in Glendale, California, one of a growing number of evangelical marketing firms that provides research to churches, parachurches, and the denominations. Barna Research Group, begun in 1984, describes itself as "the nation's largest full-service marketing research company dedicated to the needs of the Christian community." In a recent survey, Barna reported that six out of ten unchurched people found the church not to be relevant to their lives."[24]

The "unchurched baby boomers" have received the greatest research attention because they hold significant market potential. Megachurch seminars reveal that baby boomers are the quintessential consumer. The seminars teach that boomers choose a church against a shopping list of values including qual-

ity, convenience, flexibility, proof of integrity, and individual-
ity. Gerald Mann, pastor of three-thousand-member Riverbend
Baptist Church in Austin, Texas says, "Baby boomers have a
mind-set of what a church is and we have to overcome their
biases."[25]

Large churches generally specialize in reaching unchurched
people. The "unchurched" is defined as those people who give
verbal assent to believing that "Jesus Christ is God or the Son of
God," as do roughly 85 percent of Americans, but who do not
attend church with any regularity, as is the case for about 60
percent of Americans. So roughly half of those who give verbal
assent to central Christian truth represent those who are
"unchurched." They are not militantly hostile to the Christian
faith, but have not found a church that "meets their needs."

As a potential target market, the unchurched represent the
largest, potentially responsive audience—12 percent being committed Christians, 15 percent being in other religions or being
secularists, 28 percent being churched, and 45 percent being
unchurched.[26] Surveys suggest that four out of ten of these
unchurched people would attend church if asked, representing 15
to 20 million adults.[27]

Thus with its focus on change, new paradigms, and the
unchurched baby boomers, the megachurch movement appears
to represent the dynamic edge of the evangelical church. Its
leadership self-consciously seeks to reshape the identity and
direction of evangelicalism.

Who are these megachurch advocates and pastors?

Not surprisingly, they are almost uniformly baby boomers themselves. Because of this, the turf battles within evangelicalism
have a clear generational character. At a "Marketing the
Church" seminar in Atlanta, Barna sported shoulder-length hair
and a silk blazer. Said one preboomer Baptist pastor to another
pastor, "I'm already worried about his long hair." Though the
church-growth movement goes back to the sixties, its recent

momentum clearly reflects the impact of baby-boomer church leaders.

But a surprising number of megachurch leaders have emerged out of the Reformed community—Robert Schuller has roots in the Reformed Church in America and Bill Hybels comes from the Christian Reformed Church. One Willow Creek leader whose background parallels Hybels' said, "Fundamentalist churches have a way of isolating themselves, and you are in a world of your own."[28] Many megachurch advocates are semidisaffected with fundamentalism.

They are also self-taught. Most megachurches are independent churches that have either a weak denominational attachment or none. Practical, pragmatic Christianity is their expertise—not dry, abstract doctrine. One prominent megachurch advocate divides evangelicalism into those oriented around doctrinal conformity (or "talking") versus self-realization (or "walking"). Quoting Peter Singe, he expands on the difference,

> "Learning is enhancing the capacity for effective action." And that would be the definition of learning in the self-realization paradigm and would not be the definition of the doctrine paradigm. . . . The way you look at a system is to see how much of their resources, which are time and money, or the gifts of their best people, are deployed against what activities. And if the major activity in the old paradigm is teaching and conducting ritual events—marriages, burials, liturgical events, and things of that nature, then that would be where most of its resources would go and how it would measure its performance.
>
> Did we say? Did they hear? The measure of performance in the new paradigm would be more, "What proportion of the people acted on what they heard?" and "Did they have a way to do that?" And those churches are good at developing a lot of venues for behaving.[29]

Church-growth consultant Lyle Schaller suggests that the difference is similar to that between liberal arts colleges and

community colleges. "In the community college the instructors prepare their courses in response to the vocational needs of the students, not as an outgrowth of the teacher's current research or publication schedule. Likewise, the preachers and teachers in the seven-day-a-week church prepare their sermons and design their classes in response to the religious, personal, spiritual, and family needs of the people, rather than in response to their own religious pilgrimage or past seminary classroom experience or their own contemporary interests."[30]

Another aspect shared by many megachurch leaders is that they are developed indigenously. Mellando reports that over 95 percent of the paid Willow Creek staff have been trained within Willow Creek. *The Exchange* is a monthly employment service offered by the Willow Creek Association, an international network of ninety-six like-minded churches, which lists available and wanted positions. With the proliferation of church-to-church instruction, this pattern is likely to be reinforced.

Finally, megachurch leaders presently enjoy enormous esteem and visibility within evangelicalism. Often supplemented with media ministries, these pastors are best-selling authors, frequent conference speakers, and are seen as authorities for negotiating cultural change. Hybels was recently invited to serve on the Focus on the Family board of directors. He also was given an entire morning at the 1992 NAE National Conference, where he showcased the Willow Creek model.

What does it mean?

The megachurch movement is bidding to change the cultural resources—what is trump—within evangelicalism. This is no small issue, as it attacks the heart of the evangelical identity, particularly its historic relationship to theology. In many ways, these struggles parallel the battle for cultural authority that took place during the Second Great Awakening. Nathan Hatch describes those changes as driven both by class antagonism as well as revolutions in communications, preaching, print, and song.[31]

And the same is true today. The baby-boom generation seeks to assert its mark on an older generation of evangelical leadership and institutions by an aggressive application of the spirit and techniques of modernity. Other parallels with the revivalists of the nineteenth-century's Second Great Awakening are its concentration on evangelism, technique, and pragmatic results—but with a difference. Gospel hymns and anxious seats have been replaced by fusion jazz and "Saturday Night Live" multimedia drama.

Though the megachurch movement has parallels with the past, it is a thoroughly modern movement within the church. Why do these types of churches resonate so powerfully with evangelicals today? In part, their sheer size and "economy of scale" give members a renewed confidence in their faith. Like a professional sports team, these churches symbolize the public identity of the evangelical community. Neighboring church pastors praise these superchurches as providing a boost to self-confident Christianity.[32]

The megachurches also give believers a sense of breaking out of their cultural isolation, of making a difference within society without endangering their theological moorings. Until recently, their success has made the megachurch movement immune to close scrutiny or criticism. Critics of seemingly successful movements always run the risk of others dismissing them for simply being envious of legitimate accomplishments. But three aspects of the megachurch movement are particularly troubling and warrant our close examination: the movement's challenge to theological education, its accommodation to modernity, and its truncated view of discipleship.

First, the megachurch movement directly rivals the importance of theological education and the traditional seminaries. Some seminaries still debate the seriousness of this challenge as megachurch pastors continue unabated in both their dismissal of theological education and their bypass of traditional institutions of instruction. Other seminaries have developed hybrid programs themselves. Reformed Theological Seminary, for example, has hosted George Barna's "Marketing the Church" seminars and has offered M.Div and D.Min degrees with majors in church growth in conjunction with the Church Planting Center in Orlando.

In some cases, megachurches have started their own seminaries using their existing campus-like facilities. John Knox Theological Seminary is affiliated with D. James Kennedy's Coral Ridge Presbyterian Church in Miami. Ross Rhoads' Calvary Church in Charlotte, North Carolina has just launched the Southern Evangelical Seminary, in spite of Gordon-Conwell Theological Seminary's extension campus in Charlotte. This pattern will most likely expand as local megachurches evolve to serve as the regional training centers for pastoral education.

So while existing seminaries struggle to maintain financial solvency and fill vacant presidencies, megachurches are creating their own rival institutions. In a study conducted for Leadership Network on the significance of "teaching churches," Hendricks concludes, "These churches have largely ignored and in many ways supplanted whatever efforts seminaries may have along the same lines. Indeed, in a number of cases seminaries look to the churches for direction and help. It is not unrealistic, therefore, for Leadership Network to regard these churches as the 'seminaries of the future,' for they are well on their way to become precisely that."[33]

In addition, the megachurches are developing an infrastructure that may eventually replace denominations. Recently two new associations for megachurches were started, the Willow Creek Association with ninety-six member churches and the Churches United in Global Mission, launched by Robert Schuller, with eighty megachurches. Schuller is quite explicit in his challenge to the denominations. He says that the denominations are a "spent resource" and that the National Council of Churches and the National Association of Evangelicals have "failed" in their ecumenical mission.[34]

In addition, Willow Creek Resources also has been started as a joint-publishing venture with Zondervan Publishing House to publish books, audio tapes, and video tapes produced by the Willow Creek staff and members of the Willow Creek Association.[35] With this new infrastructure, megachurches are positioned to make a powerful bid for the future leadership of evangelicalism.

The second troubling aspect of the megachurch movement is its challenge to the historical character of the evangelical identity. The megachurch movement has brought the Trojan horse of modernity within the evangelical camp and has thus become a prime, if unwitting, agent of secularism.[36] Its uncritical acceptance of modernity, its legitimation of the dominant carriers of modernity, its insularity of perspective, its absence of accountability, its pragmatic anti-intellectualism, and its ability to manipulate the evangelical consciousness to accept a total revaluation of the criteria for ministry will eventually alter the character of evangelicalism in profound ways.

Consider more closely the megachurch movement's uncritical use of the tools of modernity. At first, accommodations to modernity do not affect one's goals, but merely the means of achieving them. Hybels comments,

> In some ways, the Willow Creek Community Church is just like thousands of Bible-believing churches across this country and around the world. We are like many other churches when it comes to our purpose. Almost every Bible-believing church believes in the same biblical four-fold purpose of being an exalting church that worships God, an edifying church that builds up believers, an evangelistic church that reaches nonbelievers, and a church that is committed in some form to social action. . . . So really we are not that different when it comes to the purpose of the church. We are very different when it comes to the strategy of how we achieve those purposes.[37]

But as we will explore below, an uncritical use of modernity's tools will eventually alter the goals as well.

The location of Willow Creek Community Church—an exemplar of the movement—aids in its use of modern techniques to achieve premodern goals. It is surrounded by major corporate offices of Motorola, Ameritech, Siemens, Data General, and Cellular One—centers of technological innovation. The church integrates a corporate culture to serve the emotional needs of the religious consumers. Nonthreatening, prepackaged, emotive sound bites address the modern high-tech suburban baby boomer. But where is the danger? Is this not just a modern expression of the long-term missionary practice of contextualization of the gospel?

The answer is both yes and no. The gospel must be addressed to the modern context and translated for the modern hearers. But great caution must be used, because of the subtle but real spiritual undertow of modernity. Modernity is an unknown category in the mind of most megachurch leaders and evangelical pastors. And consequently they are most susceptible to its dangers.

Consider the uncritical way the tools and spirit of modernity infuse the language and practice of a megachurch. Church-growth advocates routinely employ a blend of the managerial, therapeutic, and technological languages and techniques at their seminars. For example, the following are typical comments made during the Willow Creek Church Leadership Conference in May of 1992.

"Let me net it out for you," the pastor says as he concludes a sermon.

"We seek to provide a corporate, not a religious appearance."

"Nothing should be expected in the service. It should be a total surprise each week. There should be an expectant buzz—like before a football game or rock concert."

"We seek to get to the emotions as the emotions are the window of the soul."

"If you have only $500 to spend in your church budget, spend $300 on multimedia."

"I lose 15 to 20 percent of my effectiveness in preaching if I don't have good lighting and sound system."

"We've broken attendance records every time we've use the word 'sex' in a sermon title."

"It's especially difficult to write drama skits about God. Dramas on human relationships are easy. If your pastor decides to preach on the character of God, or something like that, I'd advise you to ignore his topic and stick with skits on human relationships."

Or consider the way expertise in management, marketing, drama, and counseling begin to dominate the criteria by which pastoral leadership is selected. Those gifted in the tools of modernity appear to be the rising stars of pastoral leadership. A quick glance at the positions-wanted advertisements outlines the new criteria for pastoral leadership:

> Programming Director, BA (Communications/Theater). . . Will develop programming teams (Music, Drama, Dance, Lighting, etc.) and creatively coordinate all elements of the service. . . Attended church growth and Fuller Seminary sponsored seminars. . . Just completed tenure with 4000+ member church. . . Is your vision to create a contemporary church for the unchurched? Maybe this married, male conservative-evangelical, seminary-graduated baby boomer can help. . . . Masters degrees in Educational Ministries and Marriage and Family Therapy. . . BA in Fine Arts/Humanities, Masters in Management. Eight years arts admin. experience includes fund raising, gallery/performance mgmt., PR, marketing, advertising & teaching.[38]

Would there be room for an ex-rabbi tentmaker here?

The third troubling aspect is the megachurch movement's promotion of a truncated view of discipleship. The movement reduces not only the purpose of discipleship to evangelism but the sphere of evangelism to the local church. On the one hand, it fails to teach the importance of calling in the whole of life, which emphasizes that one's daily work is as important to Christ as sharing the gospel. On the other hand, it fails to teach its members to influence all spheres of society across a diversity of gifts and callings. And thus in spite of an expressed dislike of aspects of fundamentalism, the megachurch movement displays striking similarities in its narrow view of the task of discipleship.

In spite of the rhetoric about relevance and reaching the unchurched, in fact, these churches reach merely the "semi-churched"—WASP midwestern, southwestern, or southern suburbanites. The megachurches have not truly faced the challenge of religious pluralism or secularity in American society. An unquestioned axiom is the assumption that true nonbelievers will come to a "user-friendly" church. But what these churches are engaged in is a limited form of outreach that will prove less effective as secularism expands in American society.

The megachurches' stated objective is to create a "safe place for an unsafe message." But this "safe place" is primarily safe for the Christian. The Christian ghetto has been modernized and neutralized, but it remains a ghetto nonetheless. For example, Willow Creek provides "field trips" designed to give firsthand exposure to people and groups that have different beliefs. Thus the megachurch appears to be only a halfway house for evangelicals who are uncomfortable with being true salt and light in the wider culture.

By definition, the megachurch movement is decidedly institution- and facility-centered. Willow Creek Community Church, now the second largest Protestant church in America and the fastest growing, is referred to as "the campus." These churches become the hub of social life and the one-stop shop for evangelical consumers. The Second Baptist Church of Houston, for instance, features a movie theater, weight rooms and sauna, a television production center, and an outdoor and indoor garden. The Family Life Center at Arizona's North Phoenix Baptist Church has its own gym, roller rink, and racquetball courts. Serious effort is made to mobilize volunteers by providing an eight-hour self-assessment seminar. The course focuses on three areas: spiritual gifts, ministry passions, and personal temperaments. The member is supposed to use this knowledge by participating in the approximately ninety different ministries sponsored in and through the church.

So while almost every other institution in American society is downsizing and maximizing its strategic flexibility, the megachurch movement has created an ideology of growth and institutional monoliths that are unlikely to prove sustainable for both economic and spiritual reasons.

Thus the fortunes of the megachurch movement bear heavily on the future of evangelicalism. The ability to achieve a dominant influence within a religious community is determined by the ability to modify the practice and perspective of laypeople in a deep and lasting fashion. Whoever reaches the evangelical laity directs the evangelical future.

Today the megachurch movement could potentially create the revolution its advocates propose. We must take caution, however, for the identity of evangelicalism is itself being called into question. The megachurch movement's uncritical use of the tools of modernity is not without consequences. For modernity is never an equal partner. Instead it is a Faustian compact that could one day require the evangelical soul.

CHANGING THE GAME

The third approach questions the very legitimacy of the game. Players who employ this strategy fold their cards, as in poker, or simply quit the game. Evangelical leaders who decide on this strategy either consider leaving the evangelical tradition or abandon evangelicalism altogether for a different tradition with its distinct rules and different resources.

The previous two approaches we have examined assume a commitment to evangelicalism, to the stakes fought for within the community. It is apparent that a religious community can only function when its members are socially predisposed to risk their money, their time, and sometimes their honor or their life to pursue the objectives and obtain the benefits that the community offers.

But sometimes the benefits of staying in the religious tradition are viewed as a disadvantage, and the decision is made to leave. This is more frequent for those at the fringes of the community, but it is also common when the group's identity has been weakened by the negative effects of the surrounding environment. This appears to be the approach a growing number of evangelical leaders are considering as they look to the Roman Catholic or the Orthodox traditions.

All groups, including religious groups, keep a tally of their losses as well as their gains. Some losses and defections are far more significant for evangelicalism than others. For instance, many people who grow up within the evangelical subculture come to reject their evangelical commitment altogether. Fundamentalists Anonymous, for example, has been founded to serve as a support group for those whose new identity is defined by a rejection of their past. But the most significant defectors are those who leave evangelicalism for Catholicism. This contemporary counter-Reformation bears our close attention.

Although this shift has yet to develop the momentum or institutionalization of the megachurch movement, the leadership interviews examined in the previous chapter clearly indicate a growing ambivalence toward evangelicalism and an increasing openness toward Catholicism and Orthodoxy. If this is true among evangelical leaders, then its potential influence among the wider evangelical movement will have a disproportionate impact on the future viability of evangelical faith.

To appreciate the significance of this rapprochement between evangelicals and Catholics we need to compare it with the way Catholics were reviled by Protestants only fifty years ago. Kenneth Scott Latourette, a Yale Divinity School historian, stated in an address at Auburn Theological Seminary that if the future of the Christian faith rested with the Roman Catholic church, the outlook would be grim. In 1948 a faculty

member of the liberal-leaning Chicago Divinity School questioned if Protestantism and Roman Catholicism could possibly be
two forms of the same Christian faith because the differences
between them were so profound. In 1949 the Episcopal church
passed a strong resolution against its members marrying Roman
Catholics. The Presbyterian Church, USA did the same a few
years later. The president of the National Association of Evangelicals denounced Catholicism in 1953 as one of the main
"satanic ideologies" opposing true Christianity.

The present openness to Catholicism is in stark contrast to
such views. The trend toward Catholicism may seem inconse-
quential in our contemporary context, but the extent of change
from established mainstream Protestant views a half-century earlier is remarkable.

What is it?

The evangelical leadership's ambivalence toward the evangelical
movement is partly due to the restructuring of American religion, which has been charted so brilliantly by Robert Wuthnow.
He found that not only has the importance of denominations
declined but also the distinctions between denominations. "The
important consideration, it appears, is not so much the numbers
of members who belong to the various denominations," Wuthnow writes, "but whether these denominations are significantly
different from one another in social composition and whether
the boundaries separating them are strong or weak."[39]

As special-purpose groups (parachurch organizations and
the like) gradually replaced the historic role of denominations,
theological distinctives diminished, being replaced by polariza-
tions along the orthodox and progressive axes. That is to say,
ideological differences replaced theological differences. The
growth of special-purpose groups, Wuthnow observes, has heightened the potential for religious communities to be divided along
the lines of larger fault lines in the society.[40] This laid the ground
for the "culture wars" described by James Davison Hunter in his
book by the same name.

Thus, some evangelicals suggest that cobelligerence in the culture war is more important than squabbling over theological differences that no one understands anyway. Catholics, evangelicals, Mormons, and Orthodox Jews frequently stand together in today's fight against abortion, National Endowment for the Arts funding, and the host of other seismic centers along the cultural fault line. For example, film critic Michael Medved, an Orthodox Jew, is a frequent contributor to evangelical publications and Catholic economist Michael Novak is widely viewed as a trusted evangelical ally.

Denominational switching is also tied to increasing levels of education. In a recent national survey, 34 percent of college graduates switched denominations, compared to 26 percent of high school graduates, and 22 percent of grade school graduates.[41] Many evangelicals change denominational membership as an expression of upward social mobility. For example, some move from Baptist to Presbyterian or from Presbyterian to Episcopalian.

What is striking is the seeming double movement between evangelicals and Catholics. On the one hand, the Princeton Religion Research Center reports that switching from Catholicism to Protestantism is nine times more common than from Protestantism to Catholicism—81 percent to 9 percent respectively.[42] Large numbers of Hispanics in Latin America and the southwestern United States have switched to Pentecostalism, which has created great concern among the Catholic hierarchy.

On the other hand, some of the most highly respected members of the evangelical elite have expressed a growing openness to Catholicism. Some examples follow. While never an evangelical in the sense discussed in this book, Lutheran Pastor Richard John Neuhaus' movement from Lutheranism to Catholicism sent shock waves through the evangelical community. As the former editor of the *Religion & Society Report*, he is an established friend of the evangelical movement. He founded *First Things*, a monthly journal on religion and public life, which has emerged as a major source of a continuing politically conservative interfaith exchange between evangelicals, Catholics, and Jews.

Or look at the son of the late Francis Schaeffer, Frank Schaeffer, who has rejected his evangelical heritage to join the Eastern Orthodox faith. He has written a thinly veiled novel attacking his parents and evangelical upbringing. Tom Howard, a Wheaton College graduate and former professor of English at Gordon College, an evangelical liberal arts college in Boston, became a Roman Catholic and attacked his background in *Evangelicalism Is Not Enough*. Peter Gillquist, a former Campus Crusade for Christ staff worker in California, now is a Bishop in the Antiochian Orthodox Christian Archdiocese of North America.

Once scorned by evangelicals, these defectors have found a new legitimacy. Both Gillquist and Howard were recently invited to speak to the staff of Charles Colson's Prison Fellowship about their views. Colson's book *The Body* appeals for an orthodox ecumenism that blurs the theological and historical distinctives between the evangelical, Catholic, and Orthodox traditions. Of the book, Carl Henry writes, "A pace-setting volume that stretches beyond Geneva, Rome, and Wheaton in quest of an adequate doctrine of the church."

Who is it?

Four factors attract evangelicals to Catholicism. The first, which we have already discussed, is a common political partnership. Catholic political theorists have a rich intellectual tradition, a strong commitment to religious liberty, and a much more articulate public philosophy than most evangelicals. Mark Noll even suggests that the last evangelical to articulate a serious public philosophy was William Jennings Bryan nearly a century ago.

A second drawing card for evangelicals is the vast literary and aesthetic wealth found among Catholic believers. G. K. Chesterton, Flannery O'Connor, Eudora Welty, and Walker Percy are just a few of the great Catholic writers who represent an integration of a theistic worldview with literary excellence.

Those sensitive to the imaginative spirit often find the functional monochromatic popular tastes of evangelicalism devoid of mystery and beauty—and subsequently turn to the liturgical tradition. "Amy Grant, Sandi Patti, and Scott Wesley Brown are now more likely to be setting the cultural agenda for evangelicals than are Benjamin Britten, Christopher Parkening, or John Rutter," laments evangelical writer and former cultural producer for NPR's "All Things Considered," Ken Myers. "The dominance of popular culture in the church is one way the twentieth-century church has uncritically appropriated the values of the world."[43]

A third point of attraction is apologetics, the branch of theology devoted to the defense of the faith. Few American evangelicals have any place for apologetics. But many evangelicals who do appreciate apologetics have a long intellectual reliance on evidentialism—the appeal to historical or other evidences for proving the truth of the Christian faith. For many years evidentialism relied on the principles of Scottish Common Sense philosophy and came to be associated with the Princeton Theology of Charles Hodge and Benjamin Warfield. But more recently there has been a revival of neo-Thomism and other classical Catholic approaches to apologetics. Today some of the most prolific Christian apologists follow these views, such as evangelical theologian Norman Geisler and Roman Catholic philosopher Peter Kreeft.

Finally, there is the growing interest within evangelicalism in spiritual disciplines, contemplation, and inner healing. In all three areas, the Catholic tradition has extensive resources that differ from the intellectualized rationalism frequently found in evangelicalism.

For these and other reasons, many aesthetically aware or intellectually active Christians are increasingly attracted to the liturgical traditions. As one evangelical leader put it, any thinking believer is apt to become Anglican, Catholic, or Orthodox.

Handwritten annotations: PAST, PRESENT, FUTURE, REASONS, CONSEQUENCES

What does it mean?

The evidence of the small number of "defectors" and a larger number of closet admirers of Catholicism and Orthodoxy among evangelical leaders strikingly illustrates the weakening of evangelical distinctives and the disillusionment with institutional evangelicalism. These factors raise serious questions about the long-term viability of evangelicalism.

Although there are certainly evangelicals within both the Catholic and Orthodox traditions, evangelicalism itself has been a distinct and important Christian tradition historically. The point of this analysis is neither to return to the hostility of nineteenth-century nativism nor to devalue the important contributions that these traditions bring to the church universal. But the Reformation did not happen without reasons or consequences; its legacy was purchased by the blood of many martyrs. To pretend that these differences do not matter is a testament to our lack of historical perspective and our growing theological illiteracy.

So when charges are made that "evangelicalism is not enough," we must listen carefully. If by this charge one means that twentieth-century American institutional evangelicalism is not enough, then the critic's point should be well taken. Evangelicals have much to learn from the Catholic and Orthodox traditions—an appreciation of the past, an honoring of the mind, an understanding of the spiritual disciplines, a love of beauty, and a thoughtful engagement with society, to name a few. But evangelicals must not abandon our own biblical distinctives or devalue our own historical contributions.

God and his kingdom are clearly greater than differences of ecclesiastical tradition. Where there is a fidelity to Scripture and clarity on the centrality of Christ's atonement, we must appreciate the richness of the diversity between traditions. And yet historically, these two basic truths—the authority of Scripture and the centrality of grace and faith—have been at the heart of evangelicalism. When these distinctives are abandoned, the church universal suffers. For they represent the first things on which the other traditions must stand if they are to be faithful to Christ.

CRISIS OF IDENTITY

We have examined three ways evangelicals have responded to the loss of cultural influence: political activism, the megachurch movement, and defection to other traditions. These challenges are not like the challenges of liberal theology or secular humanism, which are frontal attacks on core beliefs. Instead, these challenges are more nuanced and subtle. They represent shifts in behavior and reliance on alternative sources, which precede shifts in beliefs. As such, their dangers are far more difficult to see. Sermons remain orthodox; intentions remain biblical. But behind what is said and done, corrosive forces continue to erode evangelical vitality and authenticity. These are symptoms of a growing crisis of identity.

Evangelicals' reliance on political victories, use of modern techniques, and flirtations with other Christian traditions, coupled with the current turf wars, do not bode well for the future of evangelicalism.

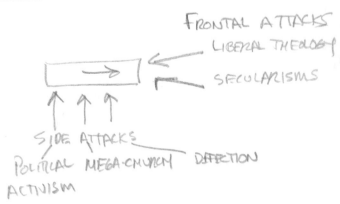

QUESTIONS FOR REFLECTION AND DISCUSSION

1. What are the dangers of an overreliance on political activism? What are its strengths and weaknesses today? (see pages 73–81)

2. Discuss the three concerns expressed about the megachurch movement (see pages 89–95). What dangers do these concerns pose for evangelicalism?

3. What features of Catholicism attract evangelical leaders? What significance do you place on these shifting alliances?

5

REFORGING A BIBLICAL IDENTITY

"The anxiety is increasing among evangelicals, and it's reaching a fevered pitch: 'What's wrong.' There's a lot of blaming that goes toward the government, toward 'other people' in the culture, without recognizing that evangelicals are the other culture."

—President of a southern Baptist seminary

DEFINED BY OUR NAME

It was the closing evening of the 1992 annual convention of the National Association of Evangelicals, the organization founded fifty years earlier as the "united front for evangelical action." After a week of speeches, seminars, and workshops, the movement's elder statesman, Dr. Billy Graham, called those assembled to face the current challenges.

Is there a future for evangelicalism? This burning issue contains many complicated questions that are beyond us tonight. But let me say simply that I believe the secret of our future lies in our name. So long as the gospel remains the gospel and the church the church, so long as the church of God is in need of reformation, the world of mission, and one last person of salvation, there will always be a future for those who seek to define themselves by the gospel itself.

The modern world, Graham said in conclusion, poses sobering questions to all evangelicals:

> Do we still hold and live by the first things of the gospel or is our faith a form of religion with no real need of God at all? Are we still a people who believe in revival or are we satisfied with the way things are? Is all we do still accompanied by prayer and fasting or have our modern insights and tools made them redundant? Are we still burdened by a passion for those who do not know Christ or have our neighbors become statistics and the abstract "unreached"? Is our faith integrated and applied in all our lives or is it relevant only in the private world? Is it still our heart's desire to know and love God above all else or is it enough to be an evangelical?

Is it enough to be an evangelical? Clearly, it is not enough if what is understood to be the evangelical identity distorts the centrality of the cross of Christ. And so what is required for the evangelical movement to reforge a biblical identity? First, we must reject our confused loyalties and false reliances that now characterize contemporary American evangelicalism. And second, as ones named by the gospel, we must show ourselves true to the gospel in both belief as well as behavior. The current evangelical turf wars provide an appropriate starting place for rethinking what this will mean for us today.

LESSONS FROM THE TURF WARS

The Political Option

KINGDOM CITIZENSHIP — HEAVEN

CIVIL RELIGION   AMERICAN CITIZENSHIP   EARTH

Evangelicals who resort to political means in their quest for cultural influence can distort the true evangelical identity by an overly strong identification with American citizenship. Three aspects of the weakening of the evangelical identity by these influences bear our consideration.

First is the danger of weakening our spiritual priorities. Without thoughtful biblical reflection and ongoing vigilance, evangelical political strategies can equate narrow political agendas—whether from the Left or Right—with the kingdom of God. From the rise of the Sojourners after the sixties to the Moral Majority in the eighties, politics has had a far too dominant place within the evangelical identity.

Indeed, for many outside the faith, a certain style of political involvement has become *the* defining feature of evangelicalism. So instead of being known for feeding the hungry, for giving drink to the thirsty, or for inviting in the stranger—those different from us—we are known instead for legislative street fights that both demonize those with whom we disagree and alienate those most in need of grace.

In short, few things have more harmed Americans' receptivity to the gospel than the manner in which we evangelicals have taken our religious convictions into the public square. Politics as a concern for justice is a legitimate biblical calling. But politics must not be conducted in a manner that needlessly angers or divides instead of seeking compassion and reconciliation. For then this form of politics has lost its first love.

David Rambo, president of the Christian and Missionary Alliance, warns that carelessly inflated rhetoric about "culture wars" and "cultural warriors" can be dangerous for Christians. He explains, "God expects us to be salt in the world. But let's do it in the context of God's redeeming love for all men and women. We must focus on the gospel, proclaim it winsomely to secular people rather than alienating them on matters that are not central to our message."[1] A politicized faith is unworthy of those who call themselves by the name of the gospel and who endeavor to live by its priorities.

Second, a politicized faith not only blurs our priorities but weakens our loyalties. Our primary citizenship is not on earth but in heaven. Though few evangelicals would deny this truth in theory, the language of our spiritual citizenship frequently gets wrapped in the red, white, and blue. Rather than acting as resident aliens of a heavenly kingdom, too often we sound like resident apologists for a Christian America. The consequence is a blindness to the way in which American history and its myths shape our identity as followers of Christ.

Geologists use the term "concretions" to describe the process by which layers of minerals build up around a grain of sand or rock to form a new solid mass. Frequently geologists find that this mineral buildup actually becomes harder than the original sand or rock. Over time only a trained eye can detect the original substance. In the same way, American evangelicalism is now covered by layer upon layer of historically shaped attitudes that obscure our original biblical core.

Evangelical political strategies of the past two decades have reinforced an expression of the evangelical identity that is simply *too American*. Evangelicals have maintained little tension or cognitive dissonance between the gospel and these historically shaped attitudes and dispositions. C. S. Lewis suggests that one of Satan's most subtle ploys is to keep followers of Christ from being "merely Christian." Screwtape advises Wormwood, "What we want, if men become Christians at all, is to keep them in the state of mind I call, 'Christianity And. . . .' If they must be Christians let them at least be Christians with a difference."[2]

This is precisely the problem of American evangelicalism. It is largely "Christianity and America." Unless we abandon the accumulated layers of American history, unless we reject the false reliance on the illusion of a Christian America, evangelicalism will continue to distort the gospel and thwart a genuine biblical identity.

Third, evangelicals' resort to political strategies hinders our addressing the deeper problems of American society, which are prepolitical in nature. We must recognize the priority of the cultural over the narrowly political in society. Many people think of culture in terms of objective things, such as television, Boy Scouts, baseball, McDonald's, or Disney World. But culture is primarily a matter of the shared meanings about how the world is and should be. The battles over such issues as abortion, NEA funding, and school prayer are simply a conflict over these shared meanings.

The gospel shapes what we understand to be true about reality. And these beliefs precede and underlie any legislative formalization. Politics may reinforce these beliefs, but it cannot change their underlying conviction and direction. Consequently, grassroots mobilization and legislative initiatives—whether aimed at abortion or homosexuality—will not stop the secularization of society. Legislation alone will not change the hearts and minds of people.

Thus we must give much greater attention to cultural persuasion rather than legislative coercion. We must accept the responsibility of winning public arguments through civil discourse. We must reach beyond our evangelical enclaves, whether in Wheaton, Pasadena, Colorado Springs, or Orlando, and engage with the national opinion shapers and institutional gatekeepers on their own turf, in their own language.

This is not an easy assignment for American evangelicals. Nor is it one that will be accomplished overnight. We must raise up a new generation of evangelical leaders who are no longer held hostage to the liabilities of our historically acquired anti-intellectualism and social isolation, who can aggressively engage the whole of life from an identity grounded in the cross of Christ. Only then will we be salt that has not lost its savor and light not hid under a bushel. Only then will we be people worthy of our name.

The Megachurch Option

While the political option is too American, the megachurch option has the danger of being *too modern*. Today megachurch advocates are ushering the spirit and tools of modernity into the evangelical church. Their goals, as we have seen, include making the gospel more relevant and the church more responsive to modern people. Taken in isolation, such goals seem beyond criticism. But the means used to achieve these goals, including the infiltration of modernity within the church, are not without their dangers. Being unaware of these dangers is perhaps the greatest danger of all.

Because the megachurch movement relies so heavily on modernity and has been in the vanguard of applying its insights, modernity itself must be examined carefully. Consider this question: What are the greatest challenges to faithful discipleship today? Are the challenges to faith primarily external or internal to the church? Are the challenges primarily in the sphere of ideas or are they rooted in the character of modern society?

Many evangelical leaders suggest in their fund-raising appeals or talk shows that the greatest challenges to the church and consequently to discipleship lie in particular groups in secular society. The basic problem, they suggest, is "out there." The list of proposed villains varies from year to year, but the top ten hit list has included secular humanists, New Age gurus, public school educators, the media, Hollywood, ACLU lawyers, abortion doctors, homosexual activists, and so on. Yet in spite of the real influence held by some of these groups within American society, they do not represent the greatest danger to the spiritual life of evangelicals.

Others suggest that the greatest challenge to faith comes from the world of ideas. To be sure, ideas have consequences. But such philosophical ideas as those discussed in university seminars play a far less decisive role in shaping social life today than in the past. Take, for example, the rise of relativism—the belief that no fixed absolute truth exists. Allan Bloom states that college students have learned to doubt beliefs even before they believe anything. Why has there been an increase in relativism?

The deepest reason is modernity—the structures and spirit of the modern world—not philosophical ideas. Few college students read the writings of such relativists as Friedrich Nietzsche or Richard Rorty. But they are the children of MTV, Madonna, and "Melrose Place." They have unconsciously obtained their relativism like one might catch a cold in winter. Just living in the modern world is enough to be infected—and infected profoundly. Relativism is the gravitational pull of the structures of modern life. Whether it is such modern technologies as computers, faxes, home videos, or fast food restaurants or such modern attitudes as progress, innovation, relevance, or change, we are all, in Al Gore's words, "children of modern America."

Choice and change are at the heart of modernity. Modern people are in a constant state of flux. They change jobs, lifestyles, lovers, philosophies, churches, and clothes with about equal ease. This modern commitment to change—and the rush to relevance that is so central to the megachurch program—is the sociological equivalent of the philosophical commitment to relativism. If modern philosophy leaves one unaffected, modern society will not. Like tag-team wrestling, if one doesn't get you, the other will.

Evangelical megachurch pastors do not preach relativism. But their *uncritical* embrace of modern tools and insights could have just the same unintended consequences as would preaching relativism. Megachurch pastors vigorously defend themselves against charges of accommodation to modernity by pointing to the doctrinal fidelity of their sermons. But biblically inspired motivations and sound doctrine will not in themselves protect evangelicals from modernity's influence. Moreover, the Sunday sermon is the least important inroad of modernity within the church.

Long before modernity changes the doctrinal content of belief, it alters one's assumptions about how life is to be organized day to day. Before theology is diluted, every other aspect of social life is transformed. The new is celebrated while the traditional is ridiculed. Big is presumed to be better. Meeting felt needs takes precedence over meeting real needs. Maximizing efficiency and control overtakes the slower, and more human, patterns of social organization. Images replace a respect for reading and the importance of words.

Bit by bit and piece by piece, modernity changes our assumptions about how we live and what thoughts we think. And like fish in water, we do not notice. And so modernity has become the greatest challenge facing the church and discipleship since the gnosticism of the second century.

But many people overlook the risks of modernity for another reason: Modernity is intrinsically double-edged. On the positive side, modernity has brought the church many wonderful benefits and powerful tools. Who is not grateful for mobility and medicine? For computers and fax machines?

Modernity's good gifts, however, are prone to make us less conscious of its dangers. Almost imperceptibly the church begins to conform to the dictates of modernity. Reality is reduced to what is new, instant, controllable, measurable, predictable, and marketable. What fails to fit the grid of modernity is no longer perceived as real, and is soon abandoned. What is lost, in fact, are those aspects of reality most precious to followers of Christ— the intangible aspects of the spirit and the soul. Modernity is a corrosive acid to the reality of God's transcendence and the deepest longings of humanness.

So the uncritical acceptance of modernity within evangelicalism, particularly through the megachurch movement, is a serious matter. For the Trojan horse of modernity will not lead first to heresy, but straight to idolatry. Modernity's potent rewards will come to replace our need for God. Our measures of success will be limited to the five senses and the most religious evangelical will be little different from a practical atheist. Like the Pharisees, we will be in error not because we do not know the Scriptures, but because we no longer rely on the power of God (Mark 12:24). The deepest needs of the church today are not structural, but spiritual. Until we know Christ and the power of his resurrection, we will be evangelicals in name only.

The Catholic Option

While the political option is too American and the megachurch option too modern, the Catholic option is *too naive.* For many defectors and admirers, the allure of Catholicism and Orthodoxy appears to be aesthetic and sociological as much as theological. With a decrease in theological literacy among evangelical believers, social mobility and cultural taste are increasingly deciding factors in choosing an ecclesiological tradition.

But the deeper reason for the attraction can be found in an intense anti-modernism. While some evangelicals seek greater relevance, others clearly long for a greater permanence. The Orthodox tradition provides the security of consensual truth—in Vincent of Lerins' phrase, "that which has been everywhere and always and by everyone believed." The Catholic tradition adds a sense of connection—the unity of all believers everywhere—lost in evangelical factionalism. If the superchurches provide sociological confidence to the evangelical believers living in their shadows, the church of Rome provides the same on a larger scale.

Moreover, modernity creates a flat world. It produces, in Peter Berger's words, "a world without windows."[3] Thus joining these older, liturgical traditions restores a sense of the transcendent for many. It reenchants the disenchanted. For a time, the rituals, the liturgy, and the sacraments bring back a lost connectedness and mystery.

Anti-modernism is a recurring response to the weakening of traditional religion. For instance, as the Victorian pieties became hollow a hundred years ago, religious anti-modernism grew. Jackson Lears writes of this period, "Anti-modern dissent more often contained a vein of deep religious longing, an unfulfilled yearning to restore infinite meaning to an increasingly finite world. The more profound anti-modernists recognized the hopelessness of those yearnings, but they acknowledged and indeed embraced them just the same."[4] These yearnings were hopeless because the Victorians were naive to the unending onslaught of modernity.

Defecting to the Catholic or the Orthodox church is only a temporary escape from modernity. This escape can be illustrated by the approach some evangelical foundations take to their investments. Several years ago, an evangelical foundation was considering where to invest $10 million. After many consultations with evangelical leaders and long internal deliberations, they concluded that the money would be best spent in the Third World, where there seemed to be a great openness to God's work and where the cost of evangelism was far less than elsewhere.

Such hot spots as Africa and South America have a greater spiritual openness for the simple reason that they are less modern. Modernity creates a global culture, but one in which its impact is not yet felt uniformly. The advancing wave of modernity will soon be a Third World challenge, just as it is for us today. Europe, Japan, and the United States are on the frontline of the church's engagement with modernity. To shift resources and concentrate troops in other places is a strategy with potentially disastrous consequences for the gospel. It may prove less expensive and have dramatic immediate results, but as a long-term strategy it concentrates on secondary challenges.

The Catholic and Orthodox churches, like the Third World countries, have not yet faced the full impact of modernity. But it is coming. Even now Catholics decry the "Protestantization of the church," which undermines the pope's authority. In short, anti-modernism is no answer to modernity. To defect from evangelicalism to Catholicism or Orthodoxy is only a delaying tactic. In less than a decade, the challenges facing evangelicals today will be facing the Catholic and Orthodox churches.

But more importantly, this is an escape from the real battles facing the church. Martin Luther warned against fighting the wrong battles in his day:

> If I profess with the loudest voice and clearest exposition every portion of the truth of God except precisely that little point which the world and the devil are at that moment attacking, I am not confessing Christ, however boldly I may be professing Christ. Where the battle rages, there the loyalty of the soldier is proved, and to be steady on all the battlefield besides, is mere flight and disgrace if he flinches at that point.[5]

To escape modernity by avoiding the cost of facing up to it is to run away from the greatest spiritual challenge of our generation. The defections of those who are sensitive to modernity's dangers only strengthen the influence of those within evangelicalism who employ it uncritically. But more importantly, the shift to Catholicism may weaken the central evangelical distinctive that the church needs if it is to counter the secularization of modernity, namely, the power of the cross of Jesus Christ.

A TIME TO REPENT

Maintaining a biblical identity is a difficult task. Thomas Jefferson remarked that for democracy to remain vital, America needed a revolution every twenty years. George Mason wrote that the blessings of liberty can only be preserved by a "frequent recurrence to fundamental principles."

The same is true of the church. The spiritual convictions that propelled the nineteenth-century missionary movement and the breadth of vision that gave birth to American evangelicalism in the forties were born of prayer and a dependence on God's power unmatched in our day. Evangelicalism's greatest need is for a profound work of the Holy Spirit. And yet the greatest obstacle to revival and reformation is the state of the church itself.

Ours is not only a time to rethink, but it is first and foremost a time to repent. Our prayer for revival and reformation must begin with confessing our false identity, our unfaithful marriage to Americanism, and our idolatry of modernity. We must confess our preoccupation with making a difference rather being different. We need to remember that our influence flows from our identity—not the other way around. Ed Dobson, pastor of Calvary Church, correctly observes, "I think we are losing the culture war, not in the public arena, but within the church. Until we renew what it means to be a Christian in the church, we won't have credibility to speak to the world."[6] In the words of Pogo, we must confess that we have found the enemy and the enemy is us.

MISSING OUR MOMENT

The evangelical identity is clearly in disarray. The evidence we have examined could amount to a coroner's report on American evangelicalism. At best, it is a diagnosis of a serious spiritual and sociological disease that makes the prospects of forfeiting the evangelical heritage very real. Evangelical leadership should be placed on full alert.

I believe evangelicalism can recover. Fifty years ago, God used a handful of evangelical leaders to revitalize a small beleaguered community that was in intellectual disrepute and organizational chaos. Among its architects were J. Elwin Wright, Billy Graham, Harold Ockenga, J. Howard Pew, and Carl F. H. Henry. Their unique combination of statesmen-like vision, theological scholarship, administrative acumen, financial resources, and entrepreneurial zeal set high standards for those who would follow in their steps. But such leadership is once again needed if evangelicalism is to face these challenges.

Reforging an evangelical identity is a task beyond any one person or group. It is a task that unites all those who seek to be defined by the gospel of Jesus Christ, who desire to see a rekindled passion for biblical first things. Some say that it is too early—that evangelicalism has not been hurt deeply enough spiritually or financially to respond. Others say that it is too late—that the church is too entrenched to evaluate itself honestly and change its directions.

However dire the prognosis, our confidence is never finally in historical precedents or social trends, but in the sovereign work of God himself. As one evangelical leader concluded, "I'm optimistic in the long run. I'm not basing that on sociological observations, but simply on the theological commitment to the vision of God presented in the New Testament that the kingdom of God will triumph. And so the holy catholic church will move forward, even if denominations and evangelicalism wither on the vine."[7]

We are responsible not to forfeit the evangelical legacy in our time. We will be held accountable for failure, in spite of our best intentions or our heavy involvement in doing good things. If we lose sight of a vision for God's church that is larger than our own denominations, churches, or ministries, we will certainly fail. If we become so confident of our own human successes that we no longer rely on the power of God, we will ultimately fail. If in the midst of our activism we forget the simple truth that just as we were saved by grace, we are to live by grace, we will also surely fail. To seize our moment, we must hold dear the first things of the gospel of Jesus Christ. If we hold fast to the gospel of salvation, if we maintain our hope of glory, and if we are obedient to his call of radical discipleship in this age, God may bring revival and reformation to our land, our culture, and his church. Such is our need. And such is our prayer.

SAVED BY GRACE
LIVE BY GRACE

QUESTIONS FOR REFLECTION AND DISCUSSION

1. The author claims that few things have more harmed Americans' receptivity to the gospel than the manner in which evangelicals have taken their convictions into the public square. Discuss the relationship of evangelism to politics. What are some guidelines we should be attentive to as we engage in politics?

2. Why is modernity considered to be the greatest challenge facing the church and discipleship since the gnosticism of the second century?

3. Why is anti-modernism an inadequate response to modernity?

4. What steps will it take to reforge a biblical identity?

NOTES

CHAPTER 1: A TIME TO RETHINK

1. Carl F. H. Henry, "What Does It Mean to Be Evangelical?" *Christianity Today*, 16 June 1989, p. 60.
2. Ken Sidey, "Open Season on Christians?" *Christianity Today*, 23 April 1990, pp. 34, 36.
3. Os Guinness, *Winning Back the Soul of American Business* (Washington, D.C.: Hourglass, 1990), p. 3.
4. Karl Marx, *Communist Manifesto* (Chicago: Henry Regency, 1969), p. 20.
5. David F. Wells, "On Being Evangelical: Some Differences and Similarities," unpublished paper, 1992, pp. 2–3.
6. George Marsden, ed., *Evangelicalism and Modern America* (Grand Rapids, Mich.: Eerdmans, 1984), p. xiv.
7. David Martin, *Tongues of Fire* (Oxford: Basil Blackwell, 1990), pp. 49–55.
8. Donald G. Bloesch, *The Future of Evangelical Christianity* (New York: Doubleday, 1983), pp. 15–16.
9. Ernest Gellner, *Postmodernism, Reason and Religion* (London: Routledge, 1992), p. 5.
10. See Martin E. Marty, "Fundamentalism as a Social Phenomena" in George Marsden, ed., *Evangelicalism and Modern America* (Grand Rapids, Mich.: Eerdmans, 1984).
11. Quoted in George W. Cornell, "Fundamentalism Storms Back," *Washington Post*, 24 April 1993, pp. D9–10.

12. Kenneth Wald, *Religion and Politics in the United States* (New York: St. Martin's Press, 1987), p. 7.

13. George Gallup, *Religion in America, 1990* (Princeton, N.J.: Princeton Research Center, 1991), p. 4.

14. George Gallup, *Religion in America, 1979–80* (Princeton, N.J.: Princeton Research Center, 1980), pp. 90–92.

15. Steven R. Warner, *New Wines in Old Wineskins: Evangelicals and Liberals in a Small-Town Church* (Berkeley: University of California, 1988) p. 296.

16. Nathan O. Hatch, *The Democratization of American Christianity* (New Haven, Conn.: Yale University, 1989), p. 211.

17. James Davison Hunter, *Culture Wars: The Struggle to Define America* (New York: Basic, 1991), pp. 59, 19.

18. Ibid., p. 19.

19. James Davison Hunter, "Religious Elites in Advanced Industrial Society," *Comparative Studies in Society and History*, vol. 29, 1987, p. 372.

20. James Davison Hunter, "Religion, Knowledge and Power in the Modern Age" (Manuscript for the Religion and Power Project, 1990), p. 11.

21. See Robert Booth Fowler, "The Failure of the Religious Right" in Michael Cromartie, ed., *No Longer Exiles: The Religious New Right in American Politics* (Washington, D.C.: Ethics & Public Policy Center, 1993), pp. 62.

22. Carl F. H. Henry, "Evangelical Courage in an Age of Darkness: An Interview with Carl F. H. Henry," *Tabletalk*, January 1990, p. 11.

CHAPTER 2: YESTERDAY'S MAN

1. George M. Marsden, *Understanding Fundamentalism and Evangelicalism* (Grand Rapids, Mich.: Eerdmans, 1991), p. 110.

2. John Steinbeck, *The Grapes of Wrath* (New York: Bantam, 1970), pp. 93, 96.

3. Quoted in Christopher Lasch, *The True and Only Heaven* (New York: W. W. Norton, 1991), p. 118.

4. Karl Marx, "The Eighteenth Brumaire of Louis Bonaparte," in *Karl Marx: Selected Writings*, David McLellen, ed. (Oxford: Oxford University, 1977), p. 300.

5. Pierre Bourdieu, *Outline of a Theory of Practice* (Cambridge: Cambridge University, 1977), p. 79.
6. Mircea Eliade, *Myth and Reality* (New York: Harper & Row, 1963), pp. 5–6.
7. John Winthrop, "A Model of Christian Charity," in *Great American Political Thinkers*, Bernard E. Brown, ed. (New York: Avon, 1983), pp. 16, 20.
8. Sidney Ahlstrom, *A Religious History of the American People* (Garden City, N.Y.: Image, 1975), p. 169.
9. See John Seel, "Nostalgia for the Lost Empire" in *No God But God: Breaking with the Idols of Our Age*, Os Guinness and John Seel eds. (Chicago: Moody, 1992), pp. 63–80.
10. Alexis de Tocqueville, *Democracy in America*, Vol. I (New York: Vintage, 1945), p. 6.
11. Nathan O. Hatch, *The Democratization of American Christianity* (New Haven, Conn.: Yale University, 1989), p. 9.
12. James Davison Hunter and Os Guinness, eds., *Articles of Faith, Articles of Peace* (Washington, D.C.: Brookings, 1990), p. 131.
13. Quoted in Mark A. Noll, Nathan O. Hatch, and George M. Marsden, *The Search for Christian America* (Wheaton, Ill.: Crossway, 1983), p. 131.
14. Hatch, *Democratization of American Christianity*, p. 11.
15. Richard Hofstadter, *Anti-Intellectualism in American Life* (New York: Vintage, 1963), p. 87.
16. George M. Thomas, *Revivalism and Cultural Change* (Chicago: University of Chicago, 1989), p. 72
17. Quoted in Hatch, *Democratization of American Christianity*, p. 135.
18. Timothy L. Smith, *Revivalism and Social Reform* (Baltimore, Md.: Johns Hopkins University, 1980), p. 225.
19. Quoted in Grant Wacker, "The Demise of Biblical Civilization" in *The Bible in America*, Nathan O. Hatch and Mark A. Noll, eds. (Oxford: Oxford University, 1982), p. 123.
20. Robert S. Lynd and Helen Merrell Lynd, *Middletown in Transition* (New York: Harcourt, Brace, 1937), p. 295.
21. David Potter, *People of Plenty* (Chicago: University of Chicago, 1954), p. 94.
22. Alan Trachtenberg, *The Incorporation of America* (New York: Hill & Wang, 1982), p. 139.

23. T. J. Jackson Lears, *No Place of Grace* (New York: Pantheon, 1981), p. xiv.
24. Quoted in Hofstadter, *Anti-Intellectualism*, p. 111.
25. Quoted in Lears, *No Place of Grace*, p. 24.
26. Ibid., p. 6.
27. Ibid., p. 41.
28. A. James Reichley, *Religion In American Public Life* (Washington, D.C.: Brookings, 1985), p. 216.
29. George M. Marsden, *Fundamentalism and American Culture* (Oxford: Oxford University, 1980), p. 124.
30. Ibid., p. 215.
31. Robert Wuthnow, *The Restructuring of American Religion* (Princeton, N.J.: Princeton University, 1988), p. 37.
32. Ibid., p. 60.
33. James Davison Hunter, *Evangelicalism: The Coming Generation* (Chicago: University of Chicago, 1987), p. 151.
34. "Evangelism, Secularization, and the Navigators" (A Report by the Eastern Division Steering Committee on Secularization in the U.S., 1987), p. 34.
35. Jim Hart, "Peretti and the Dark Power," *Third Way*, July/August 1991, p. 23.
36. "The 1993 Book Awards," *Christianity Today*, 5 April 1993, pp. 26–27.
37. Frank E. Peretti, *Piercing the Darkness* (Wheaton, Ill.: Crossway, 1989), p. 36.
38. Frank E. Peretti, *This Present Darkness* (Wheaton, Ill.: Crossway, 1986), p. 11.
39. Peretti, *Piercing the Darkness*, p. 1.
40. Ibid., p. 31.
41. Ibid., pp. 89–90.
42. Peretti, *This Present Darkness*, p. 314.
43. Peretti, *Piercing the Darkness*, p. 73.
44. Peretti, *This Present Darkness*, p. 46.
45. Ibid., p. 115.
46. Ibid., p. 256.

CHAPTER 4: PLAYING FOR DIFFERENT STAKES

1. The Hendricks Group, "Teaching Churches: A Study of Ten Models of Church-to-Church Instruction" (Dallas, Tex.: Leadership Network, 1990), p. 8.
2. Telephone interview with author, summer 1992.
3. Tim Crater, *Christian Citizenship Campaign: A Manual for ACTION* (Washington, D.C.: National Association of Evangelicals, 1992), p. 5.
4. Ibid., p. 37a.
5. Ibid., p. 2.
6. Robert P. Dugan, Jr., *Winning the New Civil War: Recapturing America's Values* (Portland, Oreg.: Multnomah, 1991), p. 180, my emphasis.
7. Tim Crater, "Christian Citizenship Campaign," National Legislative Alert Network bulletin (Washington, D.C.: National Association of Evangelicals, 1992), p. 1.
8. Tim Crater, personal interview with author, summer 1992.
9. Ibid.
10. Dugan, *Winning the New Civil War*, p. 183.
11. Ibid., p. 55
12. Ibid.
13. George Barna, "Marketing The Church" Seminar, 29 January 1991, Atlanta, Ga.
14. George Barna, "The Church of the '90s: Meeting the Needs of a Changing Culture," *RTS Ministry*, 10 (Fall 1990): pp. 47 ff.
15. Bill Hybels, "Church Leadership Conference," 12–16 May 1992, Barrington, Ill.
16. Leith Anderson, *Dying for Change* (Minneapolis: Bethany House, 1990), pp. 145–146.
17. Kenneth L. Woodward, "A Time to Seek," *Newsweek*, 17 December 1990, p. 50.
18. The Hendricks Group, "Teaching Churches," p. 7.
19. Telephone interview with author, summer 1992.
20. Ibid.
21. James Mellado, "Harvard Business School Case Study of Willow Creek Community Church," Case # N9-691-102 (Cambridge: Harvard, 1991), p. 9.
22. *Willow Creek Magazine*, November/December 1990, p. 20.

23. Barna, "The Church of the '90s," p. 10.
24. Ibid., p. 138.
25. Quoted in Woodward, "A Time to Seek," p. 56.
26. These are numbers frequently used by Leadership Network based on Gallup surveys.
27. Barna, "The Church of the '90s," p. 18.
28. *Willow Creek Magazine*, November/December 1990, p. 15.
29. Telephone interview with author, summer 1992.
30. Lyle Schaller, *The Seven-Day-a-Week Church* (Nashville, Tenn.: Abingdon, 1992), p. 52.
31. Nathan O. Hatch, *The Democratization of American Christianity* (New Haven, Conn.: Yale University, 1989), p. 226.
32. Richard N. Ostling, "Here Come The Megachurches," *Time* 5 August 1991, p. 63.
33. The Hendricks Group, "Teaching Churches," p. 62.
34. *Religion Watch*, May/June 1992.
35. *Christianity Today*, 17 August 1992, p. 49.
36. For a fuller critique of the megachurch movement, see Os Guinness, *Dining with the Devil: The Megachurch Movement Flirts with Modernity* (Grand Rapids, Mich.: Baker, 1993).
37. Quoted in Mellando, "Harvard Case Study," p. 6.
38. *The Exchange*, Willow Creek Association, June 1992.
39. Robert Wuthnow, *The Restructuring of American Religion* (Princeton, N.J.: Princeton University, 1988), p. 83.
40. Ibid., p. 130.
41. Ibid., p. 89.
42. *National & International Religion Report*, 29 June 1992, p. 1
43. Ken Myers, *All God's Children and Blue Suede Shoes* (Wheaton, Ill.: Crossway, 1989), p. 108.

CHAPTER 5: REFORGING A BIBLICAL IDENTITY

1. David Rambo, "From the Editors," *Leadership*, Spring 1993, p. 3.
2. C. S. Lewis, *The Screwtape Letters* (New York: Macmillan, 1977), p. 115.
3. See Peter Berger, *A Rumor of Angels* (New York: Anchor, 1970).
4. Jackson Lears, *No Place of Grace* (New York: Pantheon, 1981), p. 58.

5. Quoted in Francis Schaeffer, *The God Who is There* (Downers Grove, Ill.: InterVarsity Press, 1968), p. 18.
6. Quoted in "When the Foundations Tremble," *Leadership*, Spring 1993, p. 139.
7. Telephone interview with author, summer 1992.

RIVATE/PUBLIC
20

RELATIONS TO
CULTURE 16

3 ORIENTATIONS 50

4 PARTS EVANGELICALISM
54

BLUE/RED/YELLOW 68

HOOK/BOOK/TOOK 70

THEORY/PRACTICE 71

TAKEN-FOR-GRANTED
ASSUMPTIONS 72
TURF-BATTLES 72F

4 EVANG-DISPOSITIONS
75
POLITICAL
SOLUTIONS 79F

BLUE 80

MEGA CHURCH 83

NEEDS 85

CATHOLIC/PROTESTANT
SWITCH 98

CATHOLIC/ORTHODOX
CONTRIBUTIONS
101,
CULTURE 107